THE WAY IT WAS
AND THE WAY IT IS!

Nostalgic Stories of Life in General

To Crawford

Enjoy
James C. Nelson

THE WAY IT WAS
AND THE WAY IT IS!

Nostalgic Stories of Life in General

James A. Nelson

PUBLISHING

Published 2005 by:

KiwE Publishing, Ltd.
Spokane, Washington
http://www.kiwepublishing.com

ISBN: 1-931195-47-1
Library of Congress Control Number: 2004118293

Cover Photo:
Name: hollidaysburg.jpg
Photographer: Melinda Kolk
Caption: American Porch
Location: Hollidaysburg, Pennsylvania
Date Taken: August 2003
Bibliography: Kolk, Melinda. hollidaysburg.jpg. August 2003.
               Pics4Learning. 28 Dec 2004 <http://pics.tech4learning.com>

Art sources for this publication are Kris Stanford-Dony, Kennewick, WA, PS6, MS Pub 97-98, and ClickArt.

Printed in the United States of America

PREFACE

This book represents several years of work but it has been a labor of love. The memories collected in its pages will tickle your funny bone and may bring a tear to your eye.

The philosophical views expressed here are from a different era and are not set in stone. They come from a time of strong family values and mores that seem to be even farther in the past today than when these memories were collected. The stories are true for the most part. The essays are only my opinion.

I want to thank all my supporters and family who encouraged me in this writing endeavor. I also pay a special tribute to Lyn Galvin who also helped me in so many ways.

Most of these stories have appeared in national, international, and local magazines. "Baby's Stash" appears in *Chicken Soup for The Expectant Mother's Soul* and thirty-five of these stories have made the finals for other *Chicken Soup for The Soul* books out of tens of thousands of submissions. Hundreds of these books are used in the Spokane school system and hundreds more are in teachers' personal libraries. After having most of my stories published somewhere I was encouraged by many editors and readers to put them all together in a book, ergo *The Way It Was and the Way It Is* was born.

The stories will jog your memory, creating smiles, laughter, and perhaps some tears. I'm sure *The Way It Was and the Way It Is* could be a chapter out of your own life, your parents' or grandparents'. Enjoy.

James A. Nelson

Table of Contents

AN ODE TO LIFE

His hair is white, yet he walks briskly with
purpose.

The echo of his single footsteps mirror years of
life's ups and downs. Yet a smile is seen most
often on his leathered features.

He appears alone except for his warm
memories; these reflections have fueled him
during life's coldest seasons.

He has been a child. A friend. A boyfriend.
A lover. All phases of his life have held meaning
for himself and all whom he has touched.

He has been a student. A soldier. A husband.
A father and grandfather.

Nobody knows all the troubles he's seen. He has
met each challenge in life and moved on.

He is me!

James A. Nelson

THE YELLOW-WINGED, BLUE-BODIED, OPEN-COCKPIT BIPLANE

Today I saw a yellow-winged, blue-bodied, open-cockpit biplane. It was flying in a cloudless blue sky.

You say that's not a real unusual sight. It may not be unusual to the average viewer, but what sharp visual memories it brings to my mind! When I was around seven years old, my Father and I were washing the family's maroon 1937 Hudson Terraplane in the backyard. All was right in my small world.

As usual, a big Sunday dinner was in the offing. After dinner we would all gather around the big Philco console radio. I took my favorite spot, lying on the floor close to the speaker. We listened to George Burns and Gracie Allen, Red Skelton, Fibber McGee and Molly, Phil Harris and Alice Fay, Jack Benny, Dennis Day, and, of course, Bob Hope. When I was allowed to stay up late, I got to hear Lux Radio Theater. I'm sure I left out somebody's favorite program, but when you're seven years old you only remember the ones that made you laugh.

Getting back to my story — Dad turned to me and said, "Tell your mother we're going to be gone for a while and we'll take a short drive." I knew Mom wouldn't mind us leaving. She would be busy frying chicken. It was Sunday, you know.

After delivering the message to Mom, I jumped in the now shiny Hudson and we headed east toward the valley. We often drove out to the small local airport, Felts Field, and watched the U.S. Army Air Force National Guard biplanes. They could usually be found performing touch-and-go landings. They were yellow-winged, blue-bodied, open-cockpit biplanes. We sometimes sat for hours watching what I considered daredevil performances.

They were adorned with a fascinating insignie—a dagger plunged through the center of the ace of spades, little drops of blood dripping from its point. Heady stuff for a seven-year-old boy.

After watching for a while we drove down the road toward the civilian area, past all those official-looking signs that said, "No Trespassing, U.S. Government Property." We soon stopped and got out of the Hudson. Dad said, "Come on, Jimmy. I want you to meet someone."

We strolled toward an open hangar—my hand in his, me trying to keep up with his long stride—where he introduced me to a rather tall man. He was mustachioed and wore a weathered brown leather jacket. Its well-worn look told me it had seen its share of adventure. On his head he wore a leather helmet with goggles pulled up over the front. The helmet sat at a rather jaunty angle, revealing a shock of black curly hair. I knew right then and there that someday I would own a jacket and helmet just like the ones he had on. His attire was topped off with—you guessed it—a long white silk scarf around his neck.

Dad said, "Jimmy, meet Mr. Nick Mamer!" Nick smiled broadly as he shook my hand. After a few pleasantries, he turned to me and said, "Are you ready to go?" I failed to understand his meaning until Dad said, "Come on son, we're going for your first plane ride." With Dad's hand in mine, we walked toward a beautiful yellow-winged, blue-bodied, open-cockpit biplane. Dad and I got in the front cockpit and my newfound friend settled into the rear cockpit. I was so thrilled; I never had time to feel any fear. After all, I was with the bravest, strongest man in the world—my Dad. As we approached the plane, I couldn't help but notice how fragile it looked with the sun beaming down on its stunning colors, but there were no second thoughts—let's go.

An airport worker stepped in front of our plane, grabbed its laminated wooden propeller and gave it several revolving turns. The engine started with a roar and spit just a hint of smoke and fire before settling into a melodic purring sound.

It was a beautiful fall day. The trees had started to turn their gorgeous colors. Only a few puffy white clouds were in the sky, being propelled along at a slow rate in a slight breeze. I noticed a windsock at the edge of the field turning ever so slightly as we waited at the end of the runway.

I had on a light jacket and some salt and pepper cords. I hoped I was dressed warm enough because I knew there was no heater in this plane. Dad wasn't dressed any warmer but he had on a real nice felt hat. Like most men in those days, he seldom went anywhere without a hat. He always said, "A man is not dressed unless he has a hat on." But he took it off just before take-off.

The wind whistled all around us as this beautiful plane lifted effortlessly into the sky. After we became airborne the first thing I noticed was the river that flowed adjacent to the airport. I nudged Dad and said, "I hope we don't land in the river when we come back." He smiled, but I was unable to make out what he said because the plane began to bounce around and my attention was focused on trying to find something to hang onto.

It was like nothing I had imagined. The fall foliage looked like a giant cross-stitch pattern done in meticulous detail. I had no idea that I would be able to see everything on the ground so well. I always felt that the height would distort the actual landscape. It became apparent this was not so as we climbed higher. I'm not sure what altitude we attained but whatever it was it wasn't nearly as high as the emotional high I was feeling. I looked back at Mr. Mamer and noticed his goggles were now pulled down over his eyes, giving him a wise-old-owl appearance. He smiled and gave me the thumbs-up sign.

Dad told me later on our ride home that Mr. Mamer had been a fighter pilot in World War I. Dad said he had taken on three German Fokkers at once and ended up getting shot down in flames for his efforts. He later became one of the most decorated pilots in the U.S. Seventh Aero Squadron in France.

The flight was everything an airplane ride should be and then some. It seemed that I could see forever. As we flew over the nearby mountains, I felt as if I could almost reach down and touch them. They didn't look as massive as I looked down on them as they did when I looked up.

I began to realize that pilots are a special breed. They represent those of us who are land locked but know in our own hearts that this condition is only temporary. Pilots are not confined to roadways that allow you to travel only in their direction. Tell me—what land-locked vehicle can loop-the-loop, fly upside down, put a smile on your face, and have you live to do it again?

I often looked back at Mr. Mamer during our flight. He was always smiling and the ends of his silk scarf were blowing in the wind. He looked just like I had imagined a pilot would look flying in an open-cockpit plane. We had been in the air about forty-five minutes when we started a slow turn back towards the airport. I knew then our flight would soon be over. As I turned and looked at Mr. Mamer once again, I made a low, fast swooping motion with my hand, which Dad did not see. Mr. Mamer smiled like he always did and I knew he understood what I meant when he gave me the thumbs-up sign.

As we neared the field I hunkered down in the cockpit and grinned in anticipation of our forthcoming maneuver. Sure enough, "my partner in crime" swiftly descended and made a low-level pass across the field. It seemed like we were going a thousand miles an hour as I looked over the side at the ground. The surprised look on Dad's face as I looked at him has stayed with me to this day: Gotcha Dad. Now it was my turn to look back at Mr. Mamer and give him the thumbs up, which I did.

We approached the field at low altitude once again, only this time at a much lower speed. I turned and hollered to Mr. Mamer, "Don't land in the river!" He smiled and said something I couldn't understand as he gave me the thumbs-up sign for the last time.

My first flight was soon over. After a smooth landing and a brief good-bye, Dad and I headed home. All Dad said to me was, "Don't tell your Mother, she wouldn't understand." My lips were forever sealed. Since that day, many years ago, I have flown thousands of miles in all types of planes, both prop and jet—none of these later flights would ever compare to that first flight in the yellow-winged, blue-bodied, open-cockpit biplane. Today's pilots don't wear scruffy leather jackets or leather helmets with goggles, cocked at a jaunty angle. Neither do white silk scarves adorn their necks. Most important, on these later flights, my Dad was not sitting at my side, looking at me and smiling reassuringly.

Ironically, about three months later, Dad and I were out washing the Hudson once again on a Sunday morning. He called me over to his side of the car and sat me down on a water bucket he had overturned. With his arm resting gently on my shoulder, he looked down at me and softly said, "Jimmy, your friend Mr. Mamer was killed in a plane crash yesterday flying the mail."

I felt confused and sad, for it was my first experience at losing someone who had meant a great deal to me.

I'm sure he wasn't flying a yellow-winged, blue-bodied, open-cockpit biplane.

OVERWEIGHT GRANDMOTHER

The American food industry, with the help of the media, is slowly destroying a great tradition – a grandchild's God-given right to have an overweight grandmother. Almost monthly we see a new medical study come out regarding fatty foods and body weight. Usually a new type of fat-free product, under the guise of brands we all know, will soon appear. This does nothing but enforce the present generation's idea of "slim is in." Now this may be well intended, but the grandmothers of the '90s are being made to feel guilty if they are overweight. A grandmother should not be troubled if she is in this category. If you feel "slim is in" let me tell you about my grandmother.

As a small child I felt all grandmothers should be, yes, I'll say it, *fat*. After all, my grandmother was! She always came into a room in her ever present apron, with a smile as big as she was. This large figure of a woman always commanded respect due to her size, and the love she showered on me will never be forgotten. When I looked up at her, I felt adoration that is difficult to put into words. I know she never heard of low fat, no fat, 10% less fat. Foods such as 1% and 2% milk would never have been placed in her icebox. She would have considered them tasteless and probably harmful. Not like spoiled milk, but certainly not good to cook with.

I can't imagine her making buttermilk pancakes or biscuits on a Sunday morning with this type of milk—especially for her visiting grandson. This would have been unacceptable, almost sacrilegious. My grandfather would have disowned her. By the way, his name was Jim and he was quite slim. This was okay by me, as grandfathers must stay slim so they can take their grandsons fishing and hunting. Grandmothers don't do this sort of thing. In fact, my grandmother never owned a pair of running shoes in all her ninety-four years of life. Who could afford such silly nonsense!

She wouldn't have had time for a 10K or even a 3-mile run. Yes, Nike, there are still people like this, much to your chagrin. This is in spite of your advertising copy depicting smiling athletes jumping 10 feet in the air with shoes filled with air and flashing lights, most of which sell at extremely inflated prices. When you're baking, cooking, and cleaning without all of today's modern conveniences, your time is limited and well spent. Grandmother arose at 5:30 a.m. to cook a wonderful breakfast of biscuits and gravy, sliced slab baconm and eggs for those who wanted them. This was topped off by steaming coffee. Of course, smaller breakfasts were served, but I don't believe she ever bought a box of cereal. Her stove didn't have a dial she could turn to high, medium, or low.

The big old iron Monarch cookstove was what she cooked her masterpieces on, from your basic foods to apple pie with golden brown crusts that would melt in your mouth. Believe me, they weren't fat free. All this was done with nothing but a thermometer on the heavy oven door. I guess you could say it was cooking by the seat of your pants. I remember the wood crackling and seeing the coals falling as I peered through the draft on the side of the stove. It tickled me because it was my job to split the kindling and set the fire the night before. It was a chore I loved to do and couldn't do at home. My slim mother had one of those newfangled electric stoves. To tell you a secret, she couldn't cook or bake as well as Grandma either.

The fire in the stove depicted warmth in more ways than one. I remember standing in front of the stove in my flannel pajamas and looking up at this large, kindly woman, as I absorbed the warmth generated by both her and the stove. My bare feet would be cold on the linoleum floor. But who cared? I defy any electric stove manufacturer to duplicate the sounds and smells that come from that old iron Monarch cookstove.

I felt so fortunate to have a grandmother like her. I could always tell when she had an ache or pain, because when I walked into her house the delicious pungent odor of Sloan's Liniment drifted through the rooms like the sweet smell of lilacs. She called it "horse liniment." I'm sure it never cured any horses, but it did wonders for her! Another never forgotten part of my monthly weekend visits, besides her cooking, were the evenings. Just before bedtime I would snuggle into her large lap and she enveloped me in her massive grandma arms, and opened a book. More often than not it was the Bible, which she knew by heart. She was a self-taught reader, as she only went to third grade in school. As I listened intently, I knew what she read was true. After all, if your grandmother, whom you adored, said it was true, it must be so.

This heavy, buxom woman who cooked on a woodstove filled my visits with pure joy. Lest you think she would let me misbehave or have my way when it was not correct, you are mistaken. Just outside that wonderful kitchen door were several large lilac bushes. If I misbehaved, all she said was, "Jimmy, go outside and get me a switch from the lilac bushes." I knew then that my punishment was coming and I must take it like a man. She was not the type to relent. After three or four swats on my bare legs the punishment would be over. I knew I had it coming and in a matter of moments the sting was gone, but my respect for her would not waiver, even through the tears. Usually after punishment a sugar cookie was meted out with best of all, a cup of coffee with lots of cream. Mother wouldn't allow me to have coffee at home. She felt it wasn't good for one so young. My grandmother knew differently. "Moderation in all things, Jimmy," she would say. She emphasized that I must not lie, but as long as I wasn't asked I didn't have to volunteer our coffee-drinking escapades.

So all of you grandmothers out there who may be overweight, remember one thing—avoid the low-fat aisles at the supermarket unless it's doctor's orders. I'm sure a lot of them have chubby grandmas also. These foods may keep you slim and make you appear healthy, but your grandchildren will be deprived of ever having known a fat, jolly grandmother. A grandmother who sits down with you and eats hot sugar cookies straight from the oven. The ones she baked especially for your little hands. Now if you happen to be a slim grandmother, that's fine and dandy. Perhaps this was your destiny. But if you add a few pounds as you grow older don't despair, and remember one thing—when you go to the movies with your grandchildren it's ok to eat popcorn. You know the regular kind with plenty of hot butter and salt. After all, that's what grandmothers are supposed to do.

OL' SPUD

I arrived home from school late one afternoon, and like most eight-year-olds, I was hungry. I headed for the kitchen to make myself a peanut butter and jelly sandwich and to grab a glass of milk, my little snack while I read the Chronicle, our evening newspaper. Though I was only eight years old, I enjoyed the newspaper and still do.

I said "Hi!" to Mom, who was tidying up the living room, and then I sprawled in my favorite chair. I turned to the local news section and there, staring at me with doleful eyes, was the cutest little terrier I had ever seen. He had his head cocked to one side quizzically. It's almost impossible to ignore dogs or cats when they strike this appealing pose. The picture's headline read, "I need a home."

Holding the paper, I strolled into the kitchen, where Mom was preparing dinner. She took one look at my sheepish grin and said smiling, "What have you got up your sleeve, Jimmy?"

My older sister, younger brother, and I always went to Mom first when we had an important request. Dad was often at work and besides, she was always so positive. On top of that she could work miracles with Dad when it came to getting a favorable decision. I pulled the paper from behind my back and said, "Look on page 5 and tell me if that's not the cutest puppy you ever saw."

The puppy was looking at her with those sad eyes from the holding pen at the humane society. Mom took the Chronicle, brushed some hair from her eyes, and said, "Boy, does that pup know how to pose." I knew then I was on solid ground with my request.

"Do you suppose now that I'm eight years old I could have a pet? Every boy should have a dog," I said. I had heard that somewhere and it sounded perfectly reasonable to me.

"Would you take responsibility for its care and feeding?" my mother asked. "I don't have time. He looks about three months old and will need a lot of training." "You bet," I answered excitedly. "You won't have to do a thing, just enjoy its company." She grinned at that and said, "I'll talk to Dad when he gets home."

I got all warm inside because I knew this dog would soon be in our backyard, if he was still available. When Dad came in the front door later, Mom approached him with outstretched arms. Smiling, she said, "Have you had a hard day at the office, dear?" Dad was an investment banker with a large brokerage firm and often came home "brain weary" as he put it.

Dad grunted, took off his coat and headed for his easy chair. I was standing in the hallway out of sight. "Here comes the question," I thought as Mom handed him a cup of coffee—Chase and Sandborn, his favorite brand.

"You know, Jimmy is now eight years old," she began, "and I think he should be taking on some grown-up responsibility. What do you think?" "I couldn't agree with you more," said Dad in his gruffest voice.

Mom, while standing behind his chair, put her arms around his shoulders and began turning the pages of the paper. "Turn on the charm, Mom," I thought. She got to page 5 and said, "Isn't that the cutest puppy you ever saw, Jim?" Dad squinted at the picture and said, "He is kind of cute, so what?"

"Jimmy asked if we could go to the Humane Society and have a look at it. Jimmy's almost nine now, and I think it's time for him to have a dog, don't you?"

By this time Mom was sitting on Dad's lap. "Look out, Dad," I thought, grinning.

"I guess we could go down after dinner and see if it's still there," Dad said resignedly. He never had a chance.

After dinner we all jumped in the Hudson and headed for the dog pound. As soon as we walked into the holding area, escorted by a large burly man in coveralls, all the dogs started barking. They seemed to be saying, "Take me home. Take me home."

I spotted the dog from the paper right away. He was standing on his hind legs with his front paws against the wire mesh. Mom and Dad took one look at him and said to me, "What are you going to name him, Jimmy?"

By this time the dog was wiggling in every direction. I was sure he would turn himself inside out. His dark brown color reminded me of freshly dug Irish potato, and I liked potatoes. "I'm going to call him Spud," I exclaimed gleefully, "because that's what he looks like, a potato, all round and brown."

After filling out the necessary papers we headed for the Hudson. Spud, of course, was on his best behavior. He rode quietly, snuggled down in my lap all the way home.

After we got home I made a nice bed for Spud from some old sheet blankets down near the furnace in the basement. While he got acquainted with Mom and Dad I ran all the way to the store for dog food. Over the years while I dreamed about owning a dog, I had read many ads featuring Friskies dog food. Since Spud looked like the dog on the label it seemed like the logical choice. He ate Friskies the rest of his life.

Spud's adoption was the beginning of many new and exciting times in my life. He was never far from my side. Mom called him my shadow. I loved the winters with him best of all. He was not only a great snowball catcher but also a dandy foot warmer. Each morning Dad built a fire in the basement furnace. Spud, who slept in the basement, could hear him coming and as soon as Dad opened the basement door, Spud bolted up the stairs to my bedroom on the second floor. Hearing his tiny feet on the hardwood floor, I snuggled down under the covers, anticipating his arrival.

Spud jumped onto my bed and worked his way under the covers to my feet. Occasionally he licked my feet with his warm tongue, causing me to laugh. Then both of us would snooze for another half hour before I had to get up.

I could hardly wait to get home from school to take Spud to a nearby park. We often played fetch till dinnertime and more often than not were late for dinner. Mom would scold me but couldn't help but laugh as Spud tried to get her to take the ball he laid at her feet. She just couldn't stay mad at me or Spud for very long.

The nearby woods also held adventure for us both. Spud enjoyed chasing the squirrels and anything else that moved and that included butterflies. He never caught one and I'm sure he wouldn't have known what to do with one if he had. He never had a mean bone in his body so he wouldn't have hurt the squirrel and he never came close to catching a butterfly. The only unnerving encounter we both had happened when he came upon a porcupine and decided his nose would be his investigator. You guessed it, a trip to the vet was necessary and I was told by Dad in no uncertain terms, "Jimmy, don't you ever let this happen again to Spud or I'll have to show you just how sharp one of those quills can be." Even though I knew he was joking I took the lesson to heart and stayed more alert on future adventures. Old Spud never got tangled up with Mr. Pincushion again.

Spud taught me responsibility, brought me great enjoyment with his loving companionship, and was a friend to the whole family.

Mom often said, "He's so much company for me during the day, Jimmy, that I want to feed him tonight." Gotcha, Mom. More than once I caught Dad stroking Spud's head and saying, "You're not good for much, you old pothound, but you'll do until something better comes along." Spud looked up at him with soft dark eyes and smiled, or so it seemed to me, then shivered slightly with pleasure.

Spud and I were companions all through my growing years up to the time I was drafted into the army twelve years later. I remember vividly asking about Spud in my letters home. Mom said since I had left they let him sleep in my room instead of the basement. She said, "He seems happier there than anywhere else."

In my twelfth week of Advanced Infantry Training I got a letter from Dad. As I walked back to my tent after mail call I wondered why Dad would write. He never had before. I cautiously opened the envelope and read, "Jimmy, Spud died last week. We're all sorry. He got into some poisoned meat someone in the area had put out and the vet couldn't save him." I felt like someone had kicked me in the stomach. I surely had lost an old friend.

I was sad he wouldn't be there to greet me on my first leave and told Dad so when I called home. But Mom took care of this situation in her usual surprising fashion.

When I arrived home on leave two months later, there on the porch, wagging his tail, was the cutest little brown terrier you ever laid eyes on. Mom, standing off to the side with a smile on her face said, "We already named him, Jimmy: Spud."

I'm sixty-six years of age now, divorced, and I live alone in a modest apartment and have no pets. My family eventually consisted of my wife and our four children. We acquired a variety of pets as the children were growing up. Yet when I close my eyes and try to think of all these former pets, the one that comes to mind first and mattered the most was Ol' Spud.

MILESTONES
TO MANHOOD

I remember so vividly my first major step into manhood. Every culture and gender has a ritual or some act of achievement that ushers a boy into adulthood. Ask any man when he stepped across this major threshold of life. Most will say their first solo trip to the barbershop has to be a major milestone in any boy's life.

It was Saturday and Dad had to go to work. He called me into the living room and took out his wallet. "Here's a silver dollar, Jimmy. I want you to go to the barbershop today and get a haircut. The back of your neck looks like a wooley sheep." I couldn't believe my ears. I was going to the barbershop by myself with a silver dollar in my pocket. "Can I get it cut any way I want Dad?" I asked. He smiled and said, "Yes, but don't do anything rash that will upset your Mother or your sisters." I thought to myself as I took the shiny dollar, *I don't want to upset Mom but my two older sisters don't matter*. Seems like I never did anything to please them anyway, which really didn't bother me.

With my head held high and needing a haircut, I started down the street. I was going for my first haircut alone and with my own money. The silver dollar in the pocket of my salt and pepper cords jingled against my pocketknife as I hurried down the street. The knife is a story in itself. Another milestone in a boy's life.

It wasn't far to Dan's Barbershop. Seems like most barbershops are named after their owners. That's ok by me. I would certainly be proud to own a business that made people look and smell good.

I must have put my hand in my pocket a hundred times before I got to Dan's. Just checking to see if my silver dollar was right where it was supposed to be. It wouldn't do for me to lose it on the way to the shop. It was a matter of responsibility, you know. Grown-up men don't lose money—they earn it.

Dan's was nestled inside a brightly painted building. The twisting, turning, red, whitem and blue barber pole sign in front always fascinated me. Once, about a year ago, when I was there with Dad I asked Dan how come he had a sign like that.

"Jimmy," Dan replied—I still wasn't old enough to be called Jim, that would come later as another memorable milestone in my life—"That sign has meaning that originated in the early days, because most barbers were also surgeons and the red stood for blood and the white for bandages." "Gee," I thought, "I'm glad it didn't mean that if the barber cut you while shaving you he had plenty of bandages to stop the bleeding." Little did I realize years later I would look back at this reasoning and laugh as I applied a piece of toilet paper to my bleeding face after cutting myself shaving.

I arrived at Dan's, opened the door and stepped into a sea of smiling faces. All the barbers were standing at attention behind their chairs, their white smocks glistening from the bright lights. They were all eager to initiate me into manhood with my first solo haircut.

I headed straight for Dan; he was my favorite. Besides, he knew all about my favorite baseball team, the St. Louis Cardinals, and Stan (The Man) Musial. "What can I do for you, Jimmy?" he said as he slipped a padded seat board between the barber chair's arms. It would be a few years before I could sit high enough in the chair without it. Another milestone in a young boy's life.

He gently adjusted a white apron he had placed around my neck and draped it across my chest with a snappy flare. I was ready, "Dan,

I want just a little off the top and trim up the sides. I would get a flattop but I have to ask Mom first." Hopefully I spoke with grown-up authority, I thought, as I sat up straight on the board in the chair.

Dan's scissors started their melodic click, click, click along the side of my head. Soon wisps of black hair were falling silently on the apron draped over my shoulders and lap, reminding me of snowflakes falling quietly on a soft forest floor. Ironically, years later my hair would take on the color of new-fallen snow but not before I had passed many milestones to manhood.

I smiled at all the pleasant aromas that seemed to fill the shop. For the very first time I could ask him to put some of that smelly stuff on my hair when he was done. He would never ask me when Dad was there because he knew Dad didn't use it. I think it was called hair tonic.

For the next half hour I joyfully engaged in barbershop talk all by myself. It was a challenge to one so young but exciting. I was able to contribute bits of wisdom like, "Dan, did you know Stan Musial got two homeruns yesterday?" Dan exclaimed, "You're kidding me, I didn't know that. Wow, that's something." I felt all warm inside because I had told Dan—a grown-up sports fan—something he didn't know. Another milestone in a young boy's life.

After my contribution everyone else chimed in with sport trivia and topics involving current events of general interest. I couldn't believe it. It was just like I had imagined, I could hold my own in the barbershop conversation. *Wait till I tell Dad.*

It all ended too soon, I thought, as Dan spun the chair around so I could look into the massive wall mirror. "What do you think, Jimmy?" he said. "Could I see the back, please?" I said with authority. "Absolutely," he said and held up a mirror to the back of my head. "Looks perfect, Dan, and now will you please add a dab of Brylcream to my hair? According to all the ads I see they say, 'Just a little dab will do ya.'" Dan smiled as he rubbed it into my hair briskly. "The girls will surely take notice of you now, Jimmy." I scowled a little at that thought. I might be ready for my first solo haircut but I wasn't ready for girls. That's one milestone that I hoped was miles down the road. I didn't relay these feeling to Dan or the others because I didn't want to betray my grown-up image.

I got down from the chair looking like a slicked up young'n, ready to tackle the world, and flipped Dan my silver dollar, thinking, *wow, I really do look and smell good.* "Thanks, Dan," I said, as I walked out the door feeling all grown up.

I ran all the way home because I knew Dad would be home from work by now. I started to run faster when I saw the Hudson parked in front of the house. I ran up the steps and burst through the front door.

Dad was sitting in his easy chair reading the paper. I walked up to him, trying to control my excitement and just stood there with a big grin on my face. I stood close so he could smell the Brylcream. He slowly put his paper down, took off his glasses and said, "What's that smell?" "A little dab of Brylcream Dad," I said hesitantly, "I got my haircut just like you asked. How do you like it?" He asked me to turn around, all the while viewing my hair with his sharpest look. "So you did, son. It looks very good and the Brylcream isn't bad either." I breathed a sigh of relief and puffed up just a little with pride. "If there is any change from the dollar you can keep it." Another milestone to manhood in a young boy's life passed with flying colors.

I could hardly wait for the next one. It will be the big one. Dan will tap the seat of the barber chair with his barber apron and say, "Jump right up here, you won't need the seat board anymore, JIM."

CAMP ROBBERY

The day I had waited a lifetime for, or so it seemed, had finally arrived. After I had dreamed about it many times, at last it was here.

I was about to leave on my first deer-hunting trip with my Dad and Uncle Cecil. Uncle Cecil was my favorite uncle—everyone has one. I had spent many of my youthful hours helping him with his building projects. The skills I learned from him have stood me in good stead throughout my lifetime. He also gave me my first toolbox as a Christmas present. I still have many of those tools at age sixty-seven. Dad had promised me for years that at age ten I could go with him on a long hunting trip. Actually, I felt it would be more than a hunting trip. It would be what I considered one of my first steps into the adult world with the most important male person in my life, my Dad.

There were other benefits, such as the four days I would be away from my three irritating sisters. You know how girls can be when you're a ten year-old boy. Another plus, I would not be hearing Mom, whom I loved dearly, say, "Don't forget to clean up your room. Did you brush your teeth?" – although she did insist I take my toothbrush on the trip. I packed it deeply among my warm clothes. Hopefully, I wouldn't find it for a few days.

We had planned this trip for months and I got little sleep the night before we left. I would not carry a gun; that would come at the age of twelve, after a couple of years of gaining knowledge about the animals and the area in which I would be hunting. Both of these lessons would have to be learned by me before I could become a successful hunter. A State Firearm Safety course would also have to be completed satisfactorily.

It was mid-October and there was already a winter chill in the air as we set up camp. We had traveled to an isolated area in the high mountains that Dad knew well.

As we crawled into our sleeping bags that first night I lay there and stared at the fire we had built to cook dinner. As the wood crackled and the flames danced, sparks drifted high into the sky. They almost seemed to form the image of a fine whitetail buck—the one I felt sure we would see the next day. The next morning after a quick breakfast we began my first hunt.

After several hours of walking and sitting, Dad and I had seen no deer. The ruffed grouse, however, had started my heart pounding, time and time again, during the morning as they burst from cover directly under my feet. Even though I had seen these birds many times before they never failed to startle me. I was sure each one was a big buck as it flew off, wings beating in a fast, noisy, whirring rhythm. The squirrels and chipmunks put on quite a show for us as they noisily scurried about gathering their winter food supply

The pleasant tat-tat-tat of woodpeckers and the harsh, hoarse cry of the raven's "caw-caw-caw" often broke the silence of the morning as Dad and I rested with our back to a tree. Yes, this trip had become a bonding experience I would always remember.

Around noon Dad said it was time to return to camp for lunch. I was quite hungry by this time and chilled by the cold wind, so I eagerly agreed. Already I was planning a big fire to warm us up. "I can taste those Spam sandwiches already," I said as I looked up at Dad and smiled.

I was busily looking over the nearby-forested countryside for one of those ghostlike whitetail bucks as we neared camp. Dad suddenly grabbed my arm and said, "Don't look now, but our camp is being robbed." "What?" I said, "Where? All I see are some small gray and white birds." "I know," Dad said as he pulled me behind a large bush. "Just watch, you will see what I mean by camp robbery."

As we knelt out of sight I watched as several of these feathery birdlike villains pecked and scratched their way into our food supply. All the food we had left out became part of their booty. From the bread I had left open to the bits of bacon left in our frying pan. Nothing had been missed by their sharp beaks.

Dad turned to me with a grin and said, "Let's break up this gang of thieves." We rose and started towards our campsite. The robbers, although startled at being caught in the act, flew off only a few feet and lit in the trees and on the ground. They cocked their heads and seemed to smile as they chatted excitedly from their various perches. "They must be making a plan," I whispered to Dad. As we prepared lunch they became bolder and bolder. What happened next was really a big surprise. I was sitting and eating when all of a sudden one of them landed on my hand and began to peck at my sandwich. I couldn't imagine anything or anyone being so brave, just for a bite of Spam sandwich—let alone a timid little bird. Surprisingly, before our lunch was over these little forest bandits were eating out of our hands. Uncle Cecil had also arrived back at camp by this time. He jokingly said as he viewed the scene. "These little feathered robbers remind me of a few building trade salesmen I know—getting all they can from you, and you're enjoying every minute of it." We all laughed and the birds flew off, but not far. *Just like a salesman,* I thought.

To a ten-year-old these actions were astounding and fearless as well as amusing. I turned to Dad and said, "I have never seen wild birds behave this way." He said, "Jimmy, when we get back to town we will go to the library and I will show you a bird book that will tell you all about these comical robbers." "Besides," Dad said, "It's too hot for good deer hunting. We will return in about two weeks after more leaves have fallen and the deer are easier to see." This was fine with me, as I was eager to return home and learn more about my new wild friends, the camp robbers. I laughed as I thought, *Who would have ever guessed I would call robbers friends.*

A couple of days later Dad and I went to the library and found the bird book he was talking about, entitled, *The National Audubon Society Field Guide to North American Birds.* We found our camp robbers on page 629. They were called the gray jay (pirisoreus canadensis) or Canada jay—popularly called the whiskey jack or camp robber. The Cree Indian word for the bird was *Wiskatjan*, and through the years this word became whiskey jack.

The bird is found in forests from Alaska east across Canada to Labrador and south to Northern California, New Mexico, New Northern New York State and Northern New England. This bird is attracted to campsites, where it eats as much food as possible. It stores scraps of frozen meat, suet or hide, gluing them into balls with its saliva and hiding them among the pine needles. After reading this I felt good about my little friends. They had a place they could call home, the forests of North America. Best of all, I knew the next time we returned to the mountains they would be there to entertain us. It's learning experiences like these that make the actual hunting seem only a small part of your trip into the wild outdoor world.

THE WATERDOG SHACK

The waterdog shack was located next to our town's most heavily traveled thoroughfare, Division Street, almost in the heart of downtown. It would be out of place except for the fact it sat on the banks of the swift-flowing Spokane River, which ran through our city. The shack was nestled next to the river among the rocks, surrounded by several large shade trees. A cool breeze always blew up from the river and the smell of fresh water was tantalizing. The fact that it sat on the banks of the river gave validity to the sign tacked on its creaky, unpainted door, "Waterdogs—Live Bait for Sale."

A grizzled old man, his face lined and tanned from the elements, his sharp features framed with silver hair and beard, would be sitting in front of this tiny emporium in an old scruffy chair. He was always perfectly positioned so he could catch the breeze off the river along with the shade from the trees. As you approached, the cat he was stroking bolted from his lap in one giant leap and disappeared from sight along the brushy riverbank. His name was Alaska Jack. He was so named because he had spent many years in Alaska fishing and oh, the stories he could tell. He was also the first ol' bachelor I ever met.

He was small in stature and light of weight. He was so skinny, he told me once, that he left Alaska and the small seaport town he lived in because he was afraid a strong wind would blow him into the sea if he forgot to stand sideways. His arthritis didn't get along with the long winters either, he'd say, with one of his painful groans. When he was gone and the shack was closed, you were informed by a small sign tacked to the creaky front door, "Gone Fishing."

It was easy to picture Jack, pole in hand with the largest bass in the world dancing at the end of his taut line. I was sure he would land it. After all, he was the best fisherman in the world in my eyes. Even better than Dad.

Saturdays, to a young boy, were special days—no school. A day to spend time with Dad. Time like this seems to be in short supply today, in these days of single-parent families.

One of our special Dad-and-son Saturday excursions, and my favorite, was a trip to the Waterdog Shack. You're probably asking yourself, "What in the world is a waterdog shack anyway?" Well, a waterdog is an aquatic salamander with feet like arms and clusters of external gills. Believe me, they are mud-ugly. A shack is a small, rather dilapidated old enclosure, sometimes referred to as a small crude building. There you have it, one of a boy's greatest pleasures, a waterdog shack.

By this time I'm sure you have associated my waterdog shack and Alaska Jack with fishing. This being of high priority to any seven-year-old-and-up sport-minded boy. Wait a minute—I must include fathers also. Occasionally a sister or neighborhood girl would also qualify. Of course, you had to find one that didn't mind handling creepy, crawly, slick, slimy waterdogs and an occasional worm. These young ladies were definitely not in the majority.

One of my three daughters became quite proficient at fishing. I'm not sure but I think she started these excursions to spend time with me and fell in love with fishing. At least I like to think so.

Waterdogs weren't the only thing Jack had for sale. You could buy kindling, ice, white gas, night crawlers and most anything else to do with fishing or the outdoors. There were also stacks of canned goods, mostly beans. Over in the corner near the galvanized tubs full of waterdogs was an old army cot. A tattered blanket was its bedspread. Another corner held an old black potbellied woodstove. Dad told me later he was sure Jack also lived in the Waterdog Shack. At the time I thought this was ok. He was sure close to good river fishing and he had plenty of beans.

In the winter he existed by selling kindling, lump coal, Presto logs and scrap mill ends from a nearby sawmill.

The walls of the shack were adorned with outdated girly calendars as well as advertisements for old Red Mule Chewing Tobacco. When Grandpa was along he stocked up on the old Red Mule because Grandma wouldn't let him buy it at home. It would be my job when we took him home to sneak it into his bedroom. Dad said it was ok as long as Grandma didn't ask me if I had any chewing tobacco. As you can imagine, this never happened. What grandmother would ask her seven-year-old grandson if he had any chewing tobacco? Grandpa was home free.

While Dad haggled over the price of the waterdogs I walked over to the riverbank and practiced imaginary casts into the river's weeded shoreline. The dark, sometimes unfriendly, watery depths had always held an aura of mystery, beginning with the tale of Jonah and the whale, up to and including Moby Dick. In today's world you could also include the movie *Jaws*.

Add to this mystique the possibility of catching a gigantic fish from these deep waters and your pent-up anticipation becomes almost sensuous. Surely some surly bass would be lurking in the shadows in the dark water, just waiting to grab my bait with a splashing fury.

After what seemed only minutes but, what was in reality closer to two hours, Dad would say, "Come on, Son, time to go. Mom will be wondering what has become of us". *Fat chance*, I thought as

I trudged begrudgingly back to the car. She knew we were going to the Waterdog Shack so she wouldn't be planning an early dinner. Besides Saturdays didn't come around often enough during fishing season. Her honey-do's would have to wait.

Often we purchased nothing at Jack's but I didn't care. At least I would be going home with another fish story from Jack. Dreaming material until our next visit to the Waterdog Shack.

Many years later while reading Hemingway's novella, *The Old Man and the Sea*, I'd picture Jack standing in a small boat in heavy seas, fighting the largest king salmon in the ocean. This wisp of a man would be standing almost gallantly, with his pole in hand and taut line streaming out behind the boat, locked in mortal combat with a monster from the ocean depths. All the while showing the strength and courage of a tiny red-winged blackbird, clutching the back of a majestic red tail hawk—driving it to the ground, in its fight to protect its nest.

In my imagination, as a small boy I would be at his side shouting encouragement all during his epic struggle between man and fish. Due to my faith in Jack I knew it would only be a matter of time before this trophy would be in the boat.

We both knew it was a prize when it made its first leap several feet in the air above the water in its beginning fight for freedom, its massive body sparkling in the sun. The giant fish began throwing its head from side to side, as it danced across the water on its tail, trying desperately to shake the hook. It was a breathtaking sight. After hours of struggle, Jack, bone tired and wet with sweat was finally able to bring this awesome creature alongside our boat. His fingers were burned raw and bleeding caused by the fishing line as it raced between his fingers during their extended battle. He then gingerly reached down and grabbed its heaving gills and with one mighty motion heaved the enormous salmon into the boat.

The boat rocked from the added weight of its bulky body. I could only stare in wonder at its immense size. Without hesitation, Jack leaned down, smiled at me and gently removed the hook from the tooth-filled jaws of his exhausted prize. I then watched in utter disbelief as Jack gently picked up his beautiful trophy and slowly, with the utmost tenderness, released it back into its watery domain. The salmon dove for deep water, rejuvenated with the strength of freedom. As we both stared at its swirling wake I heard Jack softly whisper, "Go back to the sea—strong one." Surely Hemingway must have been smiling somewhere nearby. I know I was. Dad would have been pleased as well.

Now, years later as I travel down the six lanes of traffic instead of two on the main thoroughfare toward the river, I think of Jack and the Waterdog Shack. As I speed over the new bridge and look down at the river, everything has changed or is gone completely. All that's really left as I remember, is the glistening, churning, fast-flowing river.

I often wonder as I glance at the stern-faced drivers next to me if they ever had their very own Waterdog Shack. It doesn't necessarily even have to sell waterdogs. Just someplace where they can share themselves with their children on a pleasant afternoon, as Dad did with me. My children do.

Maybe on my way home as I cross the bridge and look down along the river my Waterdog Shack will be there once again. Jack will be gone but because of my memories, I will always have a key to its front door.

THE NAT

"Hey Jim, Harry James is going to be at the Nat this weekend. Grab Lois and we'll dance the night away to 'Cherry, Berry Bin.'" The voice was coming from my friend Ron. He and I had been dating sisters for a few months. Seemed only natural that two friends since grade school through high school would date sisters. Ron and Barb, Lois' sister, had introduced me to Lois and we had such fun together the dates just kept coming. Even though I was in college and she was in high school the magic seemed to be there.

I'm getting a little ahead of my story, which in reality is about Natatorium Park or "The Nat" as it was called. An amusement park here in Spokane near the Spokane River, it was owned and operated by Lloyd Vogel and his family.

It was the place to go for years and a mecca of entertainment for Fort Wright soldiers and Farragut Naval Base sailors during the war years.

It had a roller coaster called the "Jack Rabbit" that in my eyes was equal to any other roller coaster in the world. That first hill was a butterfly-filled stomach tightener. It took a lot of fun rides before I ever dared raise my hands over my head but I didn't tell Lois. No, it wasn't Silverwood or The Timber Terror but then they don't have big bands either.

The Boardwalk, with all its arcades, was not only fun—it never ceased to drain your pockets. You had to watch yourself so as not to spend all your money before you got to the main rides. The large mirrors that distorted your image and features certainly made you laugh.

The girly animated picture shows attracted a lot of lonely servicemen but I didn't waste my money on such nonsense. Like a popular song of the day voiced, "I'm gonna buy a paper doll that I can call my own." I had my paper doll in Lois and I didn't need the animated ones.

My first date with Lois was down at the Nat. We had a great time and I'm sure I never spent more than a $20 bill. I even won a kewpie doll, which Lois immediately claimed, for knocking a stack of wooden bottles off a table. For all I know she still has it. Yes, it had a tunnel of love and when the monster jumped out of its darkness your date surely couldn't help but end up in your arms. This always called for another ride and hopefully another chance to hold your date close and ease her fears.

A trip to the Nat wouldn't be complete without a ride on the carousel—ok, the merry-go-round. I never did catch the brass ring but who cared. Its calliope still plays "Off We Go into the Wild Blue Yonder," the Army Air Force theme song.

But most of all the big bands that came through were its biggest drawing card for young and old alike. Benny Goodman, Tommy Dorsey, Stan Kenton, Harry James, Glen Miller's Orchestra, Red Nichols and his Five Pennies, Kay Kaiser and his band of Musical Knowledge—you name them, they were at the Nat at one time or another. Their music was soft, sweet, and genuine. No amplifiers, synthesizer, or sound mixer here. Only swing music as it should be played. Horns muted on occasion could almost put you in another world as you would swing and sway. The fast ones came occasionally just to keep you—how does the song go—"In the Mood" to never sit one out.

Of course the one I remember best was Harry James. It was one of my first dates with Lois and we doubled with Ron and Barb. I must admit Ron and I had imbibed a few spirits on this particular night and were full of fun.

We entered the door amid the whirling, swishing sound of Lois' crinoline skirt and the strains of Avalon. I could hardly wait to check our coats as a jitterbug favorite, "Bumble Boogie" sent everyone to the dance floor.

I paid a dollar for a program with Harry James and all the band members pictured, along with a picture of his beautiful wife, Betty Grable. She was every serviceman's pinup during World War II and also many twelve-year-old boys'. I will never forget her smiling face looking back over her shoulder in her backless, skintight, one-piece bathing suit. You guessed it—I had one of the posters too. Poor Ron, his mom wouldn't let him pin one up in his room. My room was in the basement and my Mother, who was handicapped, never came downstairs. I was home free.

Lois had asked me if I would get the program signed by Harry James so she could place it among her souvenirs. As we swayed to the music near the front of the stage I worked my way through the crowd and headed for Mr. Trumpet himself, Harry James. After I beat the program on the stage through a couple of songs he finally relented, bent down, and said, "I hope your date appreciates this." With a flair he signed the program with these words, "Make this a night to remember." It was and I never have forgotten that interlude in my life. When they ended the evening with "You Made Me Love You" I knew I was in love. There were many dances after that moonlit evening on the dance pavilion at the Nat for Lois and me, for about three years later down the road we were married.

While we were separated during my service time before marriage I danced at many places, including the Mark Hopkins Hotel in San Francisco. The view of San Francisco Bay from Nob Hill while dancing at the Top of the Mark was spectacular. The cute red-haired army nurse I was dancing with also moved softly and easily in my embrace. But this point in time didn't hold a candle to the Nat and the view of the Spokane River, dancing with Lois in my arms.

I'm sure most of us have had a Natatorium Park in our life at one time or another. I only hope it was as memorable and meaningful as mine was. The Nat is gone now and so is my marriage, but I will always have a key to their door of musical memories.

SUNDAY DRIVES
LAST FOREVER

Sounding irritated, Dad called up the stairs to our bedrooms, where my two sisters and I were busy dressing. "If you don't hurry up we're not going to go," he hollered in his gruffest voice.

It was early on a sunny Sunday morning and grandiose plans had been laid out the night before. Today, the family was going on a Sunday drive in the Hudson. Yes, praying for good weather had certainly helped.

Now a Sunday drive might not be cause for excitement in your household but in our house it was an event. What was once the great American Sunday pastime has almost disappeared. How sad. It has been replaced in our fast-paced world of today, with parents desperately trying to cover all their children's varied events on a weekend.

Our family's Sunday excursions were probably no different from those of millions of other families across our country years ago but they were very special to us. Dad, seated behind the wheel of the Hudson, was our travel agent, teacher, chauffeur, and disciplinarian. Mom, who had packed the lunch—fried chicken, potato salad, and sweet rolls, was the smiling face who gently reminded us, "I'm only going to tell you one more time, quit your squabbling now or we will have to turn the car around and go home." She also constantly reminded Dad, "Don't drive so fast, Jim. We want to enjoy the scenery. Besides, when the trees go by so fast it makes me dizzy." We all laughed and with a smile on his face, Dad would slow down saying, "Sorry, Dear, I sure don't want that to happen." Of course, we all knew it was only Mom's way of being a front seat, backseat driver, since she always sat close to Dad in the front seat. After all, they were in love.

Next to the family dinner table, I believe a Sunday drive in the family car did more to solidify a family group than any other form of group activity. Pleasant conversation was supplemented by Dad constantly telling us about the surrounding area.

I remember many of the stories he told about the history of our geographical area as we drove along. The day we drove by a large meadow near the Idaho border sticks in my mind. Dad said, "This is where an army colonel had his troops shoot and kill many horses taken from nearby Indians. This was done to immobilize them so they couldn't wage war." Dad added, "They still find horse bones now and then." This particular spot was marked with a stone marker and I believe it's there to this day.

Nearby Coulee Dam, classified as a modern wonder of the world, was another great Sunday drive. This stone monument to man's ingenuity was a wonder to me at ten years old. I was so proud of its location so near our town that I wrote an essay about it in school. I got a B minus.

Coulee Dam was a daylong trip that meant lunch in a sagebrush field overlooking the majestic Columbia River. The smell of sage and the sight of jackrabbits running here and there would linger in my memory for days afterwards. Dad's history lesson about the surrounding area was sprinkled with an exciting tale about an outlaw named Harry Tracy, who had hidden from the law in the general area for weeks. Dad even went so far as to point out an old dilapidated shack one day saying, "That's where Tracy was surrounded by a posse and shot." To a small boy this was heady stuff.

Today, I really wonder if the tale was true but I never doubted Dad. He could have been mistaken but I'm sure the story held more fact than fiction. After all, he was my Dad. Mom would just nod her head while he lectured and occasionally add a morsel of knowledge herself, while we quietly munched on doubled-filled Oreos that we had secretly snuggled into the back seat.

One Sunday as we headed East towards Coeur d'Alene for the day, she told us the story of how Grandpa had worked in the mines in the Wallace Kellogg area. It was a physically demanding job and a rough place to live. Their family, consisting of parents and ten children, lived in an extremely narrow canyon near the mines where Grandpa worked. The canyon was so narrow that when the daily train came into town, the stores along the main street had to pull up their store awnings. Years later I saw pictures and read stories about Burke Canyon in history books.

Mom said her job as a small girl was simple. When Grandpa got home from the mine all tired and dirty, she was given fifth cents and sent to the corner saloon to get him a tin bucket of cold beer. It was a nice walk and if she got home without spilling too much of the golden liquid, she got to keep the change. Mom said she never ran. She ended her story with, "Before the train went back down the canyon, Grandma would have to bring in the wash from the line, so it wouldn't be carried off when the train went by."

Grandpa didn't have a car, so occasionally he and Grandma squeezed in the Hudson and went with us on a Sunday. We all enjoyed this added company because they always added a few of their own life's adventures and there were many. The one about how she had come west in a wagon train was my favorite. That is a story in itself.

Another favorite of us all was about the time Grandpa was in a mine cave-in. The cave-in broke his leg, which ended up in a cast. Grandma said Grandpa got so mad when he had to stay home from work that he took a hammer and broke off the cast so he could get back to work. Grandpa would smile, saying, "I only did it because I wanted a cold bucket of beer after a hard day's work." Grandma told him to "Hush, there were kids in the car."

The Hudson took us on so many Sunday drives, there are too many to mention. Each one was a learning experience and only did more to strengthen our family unit.

The only time they were really interrupted was during the war when gas was rationed. Dad walked to work and most everywhere else just to save up ration coupons for gas. Sometimes weeks went by before Dad had enough gas coupons for a Sunday drive. We all knew we had to do our part for the war effort so it wasn't disappointing.

I don't hear families talk about Sunday drives any more. Seems like everyone in families in today's world are going in different directions—soccer games, youth football, youth hockey, movies, TV, skiing, rollerblading and so forth. All of these activities have taken a toll on this great American family pastime. Unfortunately, so much knowledge will be lost. Not only about the surrounding area but family history itself—the kind of family history we all learned in the back seat of the Hudson, on a Sunday afternoon.

Years went by and the back seat that used to hold all four of us was reduced one child at a time, but not before years of Sunday drives had solidly bound us as a family.

There are only so many Sundays in your lifetime for you and your family. Why don't you plan a Sunday drive this weekend? You will all be better for it and above all, don't hurry home to watch TV.

MY LITTLE WHITE HOUSE
ON THE PRAIRIE

It is difficult for someone like me, who was raised in the country, to imagine growing up in the city, where, instead of viewing soaring hawks and bald eagles in clear blue skies, one is treated to the sight of tall buildings and cloudy haze. City nights are also filled with colorful neon lights instead of bright stars. In the country's total darkness, each star becomes a twinkler and you knew if you were just a little taller, you could reach up and touch one. If you're patient enough, one may even fall in your direction, in a streaking shimmer of light.

Nightfall in my young country world was often accompanied by a symphony, performed by coyotes serenading each other with their mournful howling echoing from hillside to hillside. Many times I felt they were laughing at me with their yipping, simply because I couldn't join in their song.

The silence of a summer night was broken only by the occasional hoot, hoot, of the owl perched outside my bedroom window. This sound was always comforting and reassuring to me. The owl didn't stay long before it started on its nightly hunt. It flew so silently with its softly beating wings, its unsuspecting prey never knew it was there.

The deep-throated ribbett, ribbett, ribbett nighttime lullaby from the bullfrogs in the nearby beaver pond lulled me to sleep on many occasions. The shrill chirping of the crickets calling to their mates, chirp, chirp, chirp, only added to my peaceful slumber.

Yes, a little white house on the prairie was the setting for my childhood. Many times I sat in my treehouse, built in the big willow in my backyard, wondering what it would be like to live in the city. It was difficult for me to envision living anywhere, except in nature's wonderland, where I was growing up. I wasn't rich in a monetary sense but the esthetic beauty of my environment made me a millionaire many times over. I had heard all the stories about city kids growing up, never seeing or touching a live barnyard animal. This was hard for me to comprehend and fortunately I didn't have to.

The thought of never seeing a robin pull a worm from a field of green grass made me feel sad. It's unfortunate most city children will never see a sky full of barn swallows in the evening, performing their flawless ballet, darting here and there, in their quest for food. In full flight, they manage to fill their tiny, fragile bodies with nourishing insects. The ballet choreographer conducting their movements in the sky never allows a midair collision. Their performance, practiced through eons of time, is picture perfect.

To be able to look for miles across the prairie and watch storm clouds building was exciting for a young boy like me. If my vision had been marred by tall skyline structures and busy sounds of the city, it would not have been the same. My excitement at an impending storm was heightened as I watched lightning in the distance dance from thunderhead to thunderhead. At times it was so far away I couldn't hear the thunder. I knew moisture would come with the fury of the storm and fill the air with the distinct smell of falling rain on freshly plowed earth. This pleasant odor would be lost to those living in a bustling, concrete city.

I would smile as I watched flocks of geese, honking in their ceaseless social chatter, set their wings and glide slowly, yet swiftly, to a smooth landing on the nearby beaver pond. Their noisy voices sounded joyful and excited when they realized they had found a safe haven to gather, preen, and rest. The goslings rolling and diving in the water reminded me of children at the beach.

On dark nights, lying in my bed I often heard the sharp slap of a beaver's tail as it hit the water with alarm, warning the rest of its family something was amiss in their secure waterworld. I could only guess it had been startled by a thirsty deer that had dipped its dainty head into the beavers' home. That would be enough to scare anyone, even you or me.

Sunday was the family's day to go to church. Being a young boy, I felt this was a waste of a perfectly good day, one that could be better spent fishing, playing with "Old Duke," my dog, hunting frogs or skipping rocks on the beaver pond.

The only thing that made church palatable to me was the ride home. Dad always took the long way home so we could pass a little spring nestled in cool shadows, sparkling like a jewel, near the base of a tall cliff. After brushing away the green floating moss, with cupped hands we would all drink our fill. The water was so cold it would hurt your teeth. Thinking back on past Sunday sermons, as I drank this nectar from God, I thought, "Yes, Mr. Preacher, all good things do come from heaven."

The white mist creeping across the surrounding lowland in late afternoon and evening always added an air of mystique to the colorful countryside. Morning air was always scented with the fragrance of newly mown hay in the summer. It felt fresh and cool as it entered my lungs, without a hint of carbon dioxide to taint its goodness. For all I knew or cared, my life would always revolve around my little white house on the prairie. But as so often happens, the best laid plans of mice and men often go astray.

It has been many years now since I last heard the slap of a beaver's tail on water or the whistling wings of landing geese or seen the graceful flight of barn swallows. The hunting owl and serenading coyotes no longer fill my nights with nature's pleasures. The stars at night don't look nearly as bright as they did when I was younger. Not due to age, but because I now live in an apartment in the city.

In my new surroundings the green meadows have been replaced with a parking lot. My night sky is now filled with bright neon lights instead of twinkling stars. The big willow in the backyard, that once held my treehouse, now has the unsightly shape of a billboard in the alley. A nearby park does offer me some solace with its space but it contains no pond full of cackling geese, nor a sky full of barn swallows.

City strollers, some walking house pets, look happy and content ending their busy day in the park. Most of them have never walked belly-deep in a meadow's tall grass, liberally sprinkled with colorful, fragrant wildflowers. They can't anticipate a chance encounter with a tiny spotted fawn, hidden by its mother, so she can feed undisturbed nearby. As you gaze down at this little offspring of nature, all curled up with its eyes full of wonder and fright, you know it's time to rapidly move on. City dwellers bear out the old axiom, "You can't miss something you never had."

Yes, years have passed since I lived in that little white house on the prairie, and stuff happens. But as long as I have my memories, I will always have a key to the front door.

PATH TO LIFE

It wound around several large ponderosas and crossed a small creek. Its snakelike appearance was almost hidden by blueberry bushes and lush green ferns. As far as my sister and I were concerned it was our path to life, laughter, and companionship. For you see, this almost hidden bit of trampled dirt and rocks led to our neighbor's house. It held adventures with nature's creatures as well as sights and scents never to be forgotten. I still remember the smell of spring flowers that lined its borders like a picturesque framework. The pleasant odor of freshly scuffed dirt after a soft rain lingers with me even today, causing me to tingle with pleasure.

Our house stood on a hill and the neighbors' was in the hollow down below. When we were young this almost daily trip meant dollhouses and tree houses shared at each other's homes. Long conversations in the privacy of the girls' rooms and daydreams and goals discussed in the treehouses by the boys. Each gender sworn to secrecy. Some of these very secrets are still being kept.

As we grew older the path remained the same but our trips were not nearly as tiring. Our legs had grown longer and we seldom fell in the stream anymore as we jumped from one side to the other. As we approached young adulthood the reasons for using the path began to change for reasons none of us quite understood.

The boys were still playing sports and coming home all dirty, with tiny rivulets of sweat leaving white streaks down their dusty bellies. Now they began to ask their dads about cologne and antiperspirant. The girls no longer were concerned about doll clothes, only their own wardrobes, often spending hours planning a weekly school wardrobe and talking more and more about grown-up things. Especially the opposite sex.

Years passed and the path began to get more and more use and we began to think of each other in an entirely different light. New exciting feelings were beginning to course through our bodies. The path wasn't changing but we all were. It started with the boys bringing flowers and baskets of berries picked along the path as gifts, to the girls' houses. Eventually these offerings became corsages and packages wrapped in pretty ribbons. These were often presented with shaky hands and shy smiles. We hopefully expected our gifts to be well received and they always were, but you never know how girls will react. It's called, "Keep them guessing." As you might expect ,our love affairs blossomed as the blueberries changed colors through several seasons and the slow-moving stream froze and thawed year after year.

Yes, our mates and now our children all agree paths should never be allowed to become overgrown. There would be too many losers at both ends. Our path is still in use. The ponderosas have grown taller, the creek a little wider and the blueberry bushes much thicker. But one thing for sure, our children's feet now know the softness of the path's dirt carpet, the sharpness of its stones and the pleasant smell of scuffed dirt after a soft rain. Is the path beginning to work its magic once again?

Paths may also lead to adventure and the unknown. Often while you walk in the woods a new path will be found. I always get excited as I wander down these small, unknown pathways, not knowing where they're going but fully assured the same path will allow me to safely return to their beginnings.

As the world becomes more and more settled there are fewer paths in urban and suburban neighborhoods—only fences. You are fortunate if you have at least one path, one you can call your very own. Perhaps it will someday lead you down the path to the rest of your life.

THE JOYS OF OWNING
A RED WAGON

I'm so glad I owned a Radio Flyer wagon when I was growing up. It was a gift from my grandparents, like many wagons are. The hours of pleasure this mobile toy gave me are hard to describe. When I rode this wagon I was a man of many different hats.

Some days I was captaining a ship to any foreign land I wished to see and explore. This was always fun because I never got seasick. I never ran out of supplies because my mother always packed enough peanut butter and jelly sandwiches for my seagoing voyage. This was tastier than the hardtack and biscuits that many sailors had to eat. These tender morsels were washed down with Kool Aid and if I was lucky, a bottle of cold Coca Cola!

An average voyage would take a Saturday afternoon and many trips around the block. More often than not, I did not plan on making port until sometime Sunday. This would give me all of Saturday night to make plans for my triumphant arrival into some foreign land. I would be met by many dignitaries; therefore I must be dressed for the occasion, probably in my best suit or uniform. I would have to plan what to say as the band played and everyone who had gathered marveled at this solo voyage by one so young. My speech to the assembled throng naturally would be a spellbinder.

Another day would find my wagon outfitted like a Conestoga covered wagon. This was accomplished after I talked my mother out of a blanket to form the rounded top. Two small chairs sufficed as the frame. My next chore was be to recruit my trail hands for this wonderful excursion from St. Louis to the Pacific Ocean. Because I was the organizer I was the trail boss. Usually I appointed myself chief guide also. This position would allow me to pick our way through the neighborhood unmolested by Indians. My friend Jack was always the rear guard because he was the only one who owned a Daisy air rifle. The girls who were lucky enough to come were always the mothers of our smaller playmates who tagged along. We even went so far as to dress in ragtag costumes. The boys wore cowboy and Davy Crocket coonskin hats and the girls wore their moms' long print dresses, and grandmas' aprons and sunbonnets. We all looked straight out of a wagon train.

I'm sure the young girls of today would demand equal status when it comes to jobs and positions of authority on this trip west. These problems never arose back then because no one had heard about being politically correct. What a blessing. Whoever heard of a female wagonmaster anyway?

If space travel had been envisioned at this time I'm sure my wagon would have traveled throughout space, visiting one planet after another, conquering anything that threatened me or my family and friends. We would have made Star Wars and Captain Kirk look like amateurs. Of course I would have been the captain. After all, it was my wagon.

Because there was no such thing as a wagon wash, it was easy to spend a summer afternoon washing and polishing my wagon. I had named it Big Red for its color and felt it was only proper that I keep it clean and waxed. On more than one occasion I was scolded for using my father's auto wax without his permission. Mom didn't like me using her towels either. One seldom has time to wait for one's dad to come home from work to ask for his approval or to try and cajole one'smom into letting one use her towels. After all, Saturdays go by too quickly in the first place.

Yes, all anyone needed in those days was a Red Flyer wagon and a child's imagination to have the time of their lives. Television was not an option and for that I am thankful. After all, why view someone else's adventures and fantasies when you can live your own. I know as my grandchildren get older it will be my privilege to make sure they have a wagon. Just as my grandparents provided mine.

Their travels will be limited only by their imaginations. This imagination will be better honed by reading, listening, and observing the world around them. If this article has tickled your memory, then I know you enjoyed your childhood as much as I did. Bet you owned a red wagon too!

GRANDMA'S HOUSE

It was old, yet new—it was Spartan, yet grand. It looked stark and cold to many but in my mind's eye it generated warmth and love. It was Grandma's house. At this time in my young life, I was sure, no finer house existed anywhere in the world.

A large bay window in the front room viewed the most elegant front porch one could imagine, from its ivy-covered pillars to the broad, long front steps leading to the oaken front door. The porch seemed to beckon you with the words "This is a grandma's house." The top step had a squeak all its own that seemed to say "Welcome," or words to that effect.

All the rooms had high-beamed ceilings, which made them difficult to heat in our wintry climate. It didn't matter to Grandma. She always said it made her feel like she was living in a castle. Certainly this was easy to imagine for a small boy.

Her dream home was heated by central heating, meaning a large, round, black woodstove sitting in the middle of the living room. Its cavernous, clanging double doors welcomed each tamarack log inserted in its throat with snapping sparks and crackling sounds of warmth.

The living room was Grandpa's favorite. I remember so vividly, as a child, watching him rocking in his chair at the end of the day, the only time he had to sit in it. Later in the evening, the twilight shadows slowly crept across the living room's linoleum-covered floor, eventually creating a silhouette of this kindly man. Flames inside the woodstove reflected through its tiny window and danced upon his weathered features.

The crackling and popping of burning tamarack only added to his mystique as he slowly rocked back and forth. I always waited with anticipation for that slight squeak that I knew would come from the rocker's wired joint as he completed his backward motion. In my mind, it added character to his melodic rocking—wump-wump-squeak.

He never sat in his chair for long before Susie, his German shorthaired pointer, who never pointed at anything except her dog dish, was at his side. She knew it was only a matter of time before his hand would reach and find her with his soft touch. This dog, whom he often referred to as "that old pot hound" always looked up at him with adoration and wagging tail, knowing full well she would be sleeping by his bed that night.

The only time his chair was moved was on Saturday night. He would take it to the front room and set it next to a small table radio, encased in a beautiful maple cabinet. There was no built-in stereo system in this house, thank you. There he rocked while laughing at the satirical humor of Amos and Andy. The rest of the family retreated to the living room so they wouldn't have to hear him say in his gruffest voice, "Shush now, I'm trying to listen."

This scene is etched in my memory forever, along with my love for both my grandparents. Every child should have the opportunity to develop a bond with his or her grandparents. After all, they are an extension of your own life.

Grandma's favorite room and mine too, of course, was the kitchen with adjoining pantry. The pantry with the icebox at the back was another adventure for a grandchild. Yes, I still call our refrigerator an icebox. This always brings a smile to my children's faces. It's only natural.

The big old iron Monarch cookstove was what she cooked her masterpieces on, from your basic foods to apple pie with golden brown crusts that would melt in you mouth. Believe me, they weren't fat free. All this was done with nothing but a thermometer on the heavy oven door. I guess you could say it was cooking by the seat of your pants. I remember the wood crackling and seeing the coals falling as I peered through the draft on the side of the stove. It tickled me because it was my job to split the kindling and set the fire the night before. It was a chore I loved to do and couldn't do at home. Mom had an electric stove. She couldn't cook as well as Grandma either.

The Monarch stove was stoked up for double duty on baking day. It not only provided heat for Grandma's goodies but hot water for the weekly wash as well. If I was visiting, my job was to keep its flaming hunger satisfied with wooden mill ends. I was glad to do it because I knew at the end of the wash Grandma and I would sit down for a coffee break.

I didn't get coffee at home but Grandma felt a cup of coffee with lots of cream and a spoonfull of sugar wouldn't hurt a grandchild. I was told not to volunteer any information to Mom about our coffee klatches but if asked, not to lie about it. *Fat chance of that, Grandma,* I thought, as a grin spread across my face. A large plate of sugar cookies was always on the table at the same time. Grandson was in seventh heaven.

The fire in the stove depicted warmth in more ways than one. I remember standing in front of the stove in my flannel pajamas and looking up at this large, kindly woman, absorbing the warmth generated by her and the stove. My bare feet would be cold on the linoleum-carpeted floor, but who cared. I defy any electric stove manufacturer to duplicate the sounds and smells that came from that old iron Monarch cookstove.

Grandmother arose at five thirty each morning to cook a wonderful breakfast of biscuits and gravy, sliced slab bacon, and of course, eggs for those who wanted them. This was topped off with steaming coffee. Grandpa always saucered and blew on his to cool it. When I told Mom about Grandpa's actions, she said they weren't mannerly. Maybe not, Mom, but it sure looked like fun to me. Of course, smaller breakfasts were served, but I don't believe she ever bought a box of cereal. She didn't turn a dial to high, medium, or low on her stove. She only had to ask, "Jimmy, please get me some more wood."

This heavy buxom woman filled my heart with pure joy till the day she went to heaven. I can still remember the odor of fresh-baked bread wafting through each room of this giant old house on baking day. This always meant a week's supply of sugar cookies would be in the cookie jar for visiting grandchildren. Occasionally the sharp smell of Sloan's liniment mingled in with the other more pleasant odors that filled her kitchen. I knew then Grandma had an ache or pain she was treating. She called it horse liniment. This always made me laugh.

Another never forgotten part of my monthly weekend visits, besides her cooking, were the evenings. Just before bedtime I snuggled into her large lap. While I was enveloped in her massive arms, she opened a book. More often than not it was the Bible, which she knew by heart. She was a self-taught reader, since she only went to the third grade in school. As I listened intently, I knew what she read was true. After all, if your grandmother whom you adored said it was true, it must be so.

The old house had an upstairs that was even more difficult to heat but no one seemed to care. All of its large bedrooms had huge walk-in closets and each had a long dangling cord with a switch on the end, hanging from the light fixture. It wasn't hard to find the switch in the closet's darkness, because it always hit you square in the eye when you walked in—wham—damn. What better place for a grandson or granddaughter to spend a rainy afternoon, pretending they were all grown-up in their very own make-believe house. It wouldn't have been any fun if we'd to manipulate sliding or accordion doors in a tiny space—like most closets in the average house of today.

Yes, this home would have many drawbacks in today's fast-moving world but in my eyes it was pure elegance—occupied by the two people I loved very dearly, Grandma and Grandpa.

A TOOL BOX CHRISTMAS

"Jimmy, put that hammer down. You've done enough damage to the cabinets in the kitchen," Mom, her arms full of groceries, yelled as she came in the front door. She had caught me in the act, practicing with one of the tools I had received for Christmas. Like every young boy, I will never forget my first toolbox. Today it probably wouldn't be unusual for a girl to ask for one.

Dad had asked me a couple of months before Christmas what I would like to find under the tree on Christmas morning. I was only seven and a million things went through my head. You know how it goes when you're seven and it's two months before Christmas

I had already given some thought to a toolbox. What seven-year-old boy hasn't? My Uncle Cecil was a builder, single, and often said I was like a son to him. He would take me along on some of his projects and I had taken an immediate liking to the smell of sawdust and fresh-cut lumber. He had even gone so far as to give me specific jobs to do at his job site. He made me feel so grown-up. Even more so at the end of the day when he'd flip me a silver dollar and say, "Good job, Jimmy."

He was always so patient with me. He would take the time to double-check all my important measurements and level settings. When he found a mistake, a gentle reminder is all I received. At the end of the day when we were cleaning up he often said, "Keep learning, Jimmy, and you will build your own house someday." A lot of good can be said for a strong extended family.

Now you know the main reason why I wanted a toolbox for Christmas. I also felt that if I had my own tools I could do more work. Then perhaps I could earn two silver dollars before the end of the working day with Uncle Cecil. By the way, he was my Mom's brother and my favorite uncle.

I learned years later how much trouble Dad went to for my toolbox Christmas. Seems like Mom and Dad had several serious discussions about what I should and shouldn't receive in the way of tools. I found this surprising, because as any seven-year-old boy knows there aren't any tools he can't handle. Mom had put her foot down on a plane. She felt I could cause too much noiseless damage before she heard me and came running to "protect" whatever it was I was working on. In her mind's eye there wouldn't be anything safe, unless it was high upon a shelf or tucked away in a dark closet. I learned later she finally relented on my possessing several other tools or "weapons" as she called them, after many discussions with Uncle Cecil. He had been quick to point out to her how responsible I had become.

Yes, Christmas finally arrived after weeks of anxious waiting. I was pretty sure the toolbox would be under the tree. One evening the week before I had seen Dad take a large unwrapped box out of the Hudson after he arrived home from work. On one end was printed "Sears Roebuck." I hurriedly replaced the curtains and ducked out of sight from the window I was peeking out of, confident he hadn't seen me.

I was so sure it was the toolbox I went upstairs to my room and made room for its arrival. I would put it at the foot of my bed. Right next to my old toy box. Yes, I really was growing up, I thought —my own tools and everything, right next to my toys.

Christmas morning finally arrived just like my parents said it would and I was the first one out of bed, I thought. I tiptoed downstairs to view the lighted tree surrounded by a large pile of gifts. They were nestled and half hidden beneath the tree's bright lights and spreading boughs. Off in a hallway I saw Mom and Dad standing in the shadows, smiling, arms around each other. Being as quiet as a little elf, I pretended I didn't see them.

My eyes scanned the early morning Christmas scene quickly and there it was. A large box, but bigger than the one I had seen in Dad's arms. It had been wrapped with a mother's love in bright red and white Santa Claus paper. It was topped off with a big red ribbon tied in a large bow. "For Jimmy—From Santa," was printed across the top.

With child-like gusto I began to unwrap my gift, all the while sneaking an occasional look at Mom and Dad in their hiding place. Sure enough, it was my toolbox. Uncle Cecil, I found out later, built the box. It was a beauty. It was made of oak and finished with a warm, rich look. When I opened the lid, there lay the most complete set of tools any boy could ever want. They had been in the large Sears box I had seen earlier.

At this time Mom and Dad both emerged from the shadows still holding hands. Dad said, "Merry Christmas, son" and Mom simply touched my arm and said, "I finally gave in to your Dad and your Uncle Cecil. Merry Christmas, Jimmy."

At this moment in time with all our arms around each other I swear I heard a laughing voice off in the distance exclaim, "Merry Christmas to all and to all a good night" – especially to Uncle Cecil.

THE TEACHER WHO MADE A DIFFERENCE

As I drove by Logan Elementary school it reminded me of a colored cement fortress. Like something out of Star Trek. Certainly not like the tall, stately brick building I entered every school day for eight years.

But what can you expect fifty years after graduation? Miss Rapp standing in front of my sixth-grade class? Everyone has a favorite teacher. The one that stands out foremost in their minds. The one whose personality and teaching methods made a real difference in their lives. My favorite teacher was my sixth-grade teacher in the early '40's at Logan—Miss Elizabeth Rapp. She was short, wiry, with sharp, craggy features. Her voice also sounded like thunder when she was angry. This same voice in its normal tone was a joy to hear for those who were eager to learn. Most children in school have an appetite for learning, but it takes a special teacher to feed that appetite so they can grow intellectually as well as physically. We teasingly spoke behind her back about her old-maid status and I'm sure she knew this. This didn't matter to her because all of us were her children. Her job was not to raise us, but to educate us on her particular rung of the ladder as we climbed to adulthood.

This fiery little woman had a heart of gold and her teaching methods were simple. Pay attention, study hard, and be observant. "Everything in life offers you a learning experience," she used to say. She commanded total respect in her class. This meant, among other things, no whispering or gum chewing. For the gum chewing infraction you had to place it behind your ear for the rest of the day if you were caught. She sent spelling homework home every night. Nine words that had to be copied three times each, along with different spelling rules contained in verses. On the one hand it was a tasteless chore, but on the other it was rewarding and fun. We all knew we were learning. She drilled us in phonics till we excelled. I am a good speller to this day because of her tenacity about homework and the ability to create an atmosphere that made me want to learn.

She tested us daily and the competition was always keen. If you got 100 percent every day for a week, you were allowed to help her clean the blackboard on Friday afternoon. This also meant you saw a human side of her that some did not have the opportunity to observe. After the blackboard was cleaned she would sit down and share with you the licorice she always kept in the top drawer of her desk. Along with this treat always came the words "Jimmy, if you ever need extra help don't be afraid to ask." She said this to all the students. We all grew weary of multiplication flash cards, but none of us will ever forget them!

She would tolerate some daydreaming, but if you were caught looking out the window too often, a scolding was sure to be forthcoming. She knew most of us through our parents, not because of the PTA meetings, but due to the fact thatshe had usually taught at least one of them. Families were not as migratory then as they are now. She never failed to mention how upset my Dad—who had been one of her students—would be if I didn't study hard and try to be the best that I could be. This was long before the U.S. Army commercial, "Be all that you can be." Perhaps the writer of this commercial once sat in her classroom. Her confidence was contagious as she stood before us and stated, "Each of you will leave this classroom with the knowledge that you can succeed in anything you put your mind to."

Miss Rapp was also a master at saving the school district money. She never passed out a complete tablet to a student. Sheets were doled out one at a time at test time. Her coup de grace was when she added water to the inkwells with a teaspoon to save on ink. I'm sure her class was the only one in the school using watered-down ink. It would be nice to have more like her in the system today. What a woman.

I haven't been in an elementary school in years, but I like to think that there are many Miss Rapps teaching sixth grades all over the world. I'm sure few would be short, wiry, and wear their hair up in a bun. But one thing for sure. They would all have her desire to open the eyes of their pupils to the wonderful world of learning.

No one would have dared wear a baseball hat in her classroom. She would have none of that type of "foolishness!" Your parents would certainly not listen to you complain about her classroom demeanor or her teaching methods, since she knew most of them firsthand. She also taught us to make a final "t" in words ending in "t" in her penmanship class because in her words "It will make your handwriting appear more businesslike." Unfortunately, computers don't have a final "t" key.

I had looked forward with a tinge of fear at the start of my sixth grade year. Stories were common about her firmness. This fear soon faded as we all realized that she was a tough teacher, but above all she was fair. Her philosophy was quite simple. Do as she instructed and you would learn. Inattention or "foolishness" as she called it would lead to the only corporal punishment she knew how to administer and administer she did. She would reach for her ruler and request that you extend your hands, palms up. As the ruler struck home it stung, but you seldom misbehaved again. I think most of the boys in the class were corrected at least once during the year by this method of punishment. We all wore this experience like a badge of courage. We knew we had it coming and regarded it as only fair. There is something about the philosophy of fairness. You seldom hold a grudge and your respect for the person who deals out the punishment is rarely shaken.

Major behavior infractions were met with a trip to the principal's office. There, corporal punishment was administrated with the "Big Paddle." No underlying psychological problems were addressed, examined, or felt justified. As for the ACLU, Ms. Rapp would have used only one word to describe these "scalawags"—her favorite explicit "Pshwah."

The most important factor at this age was when you got in trouble at school, you also got in trouble at home—though it's hard to believe. Lack of support from home has to be one of the major problems facing educators today. Many feel it is the most important one to solve.

Like most kids, out of class we made fun of her mannerisms. But none of us would have traded her as a teacher. It was with bravado that we told other students we were in Miss Rapp's class. Some could even make it sound like we had been to hell and back, if we had known what that phrase meant!

Before the year was out we learned she really didn't have eyes in the back of her head, as we all thought. She was only watching us through the reflection on her wide, oval glasses, as she wrote on the blackboard with her back to us. So there really was a simple explanation for her uncanny ability to catch someone doing something they shouldn't. This was a relief. She really was human after all!

The schools today no longer have those neat tiny desks row upon row one in front of the other—the ones with indentations for pencils and built-in ink wells at the top. Little girls' pigtails were often dipped in these pools of black ink while they sat unknowingly at attention at the desk in front of you. The indentions meant for pencils became reciprocals for secret treasures and occasionally forbidden spitballs. Just being caught with these weapons was a palms-up, ruler-slapping offense. Yes, the desks are gone, but I like to believe there are still thousands of Miss Rapps still in the classrooms. They will continue to make a difference in children's lives even if they don't teach their pupils how to make a final "t."

THE ICEMAN
NO LONGER COMETH

You scratch your head as you go over the blueprints for the family's new dream home. The wife wants a walk-in freezer in the basement as well as a built-in space for a large colored refrigerator in the kitchen. Because you're a good husband, you must pay attention to these honey-do's. The plans will have to be changed to accommodate these new innovations. As you draw in these modifications, your mind drifts back to your childhood.

"Here they come. Here they come," we all shouted in unison as we jumped up and down excitedly. The glee in our voices was almost drowned out by the barking of the neighborhood dogs that had also joined our small group. We had been waiting patiently for almost an hour in the hot July sun. It had seemed like an eternity to me and my friends sitting on the curb near my house. At last, they were here.

What could possibly have held the attention of this gathering of young children, ages five to twelve, for so long? We could have been playing ball, hopscotch, mumblety-peg or even helping Mom with her endless kitchen chores. Not to mention mowing the lawn that Dad said had to be done before he returned home from work. But this was Wednesday afternoon and today, "they" were coming. This meant all other things could wait, even our trip to the pool. He would be sitting on the wagon seat, perched in front of a bright, colorful, yellow wagon. Dolly, his horse, would be pulling the wagon, in her slow, methodical plodding gait, bringing them closer to us with each determined step. The ice blue lettering on the side of the wagon literally shouted Diamond Ice and Fuel, along with a cool picture of a sparkling diamond. Yes, it was the iceman. A burly, friendly, smiling person, bringing coolness and freshness to our neighborhood. His own warmth was just an additional benefit on a hot, humid summer day. His wagon was full of large blocks of ice that looked like icebergs adrift in a sea of sawdust, put there to help keep the ice cool. We could hear the wagon creaking under its heavy load as it neared our location on the curb. This vision always caused shivers to run up and down the spines of our small bodies, tanned by the summer sun. For we knew Dolly would soon be stopping at our corner, without even so much as a whoa from her driver. She knew every customer on the iceman's route and we all knew her. She was a big bay mare with a white star on her forehead. Dad told me that it was called a blaze but it looked like a star to me, so that's what I called it.

During our wait we had gathered grass and wild clover for Dolly's anticipated arrival. We knew she would be expecting this little snack. It was like her grass break, instead of a coffee break, earned by her hard labor. Besides, aren't horses always hungry? "Take my grass first, Dolly, take mine," we would shout, as she lowered her head and gingerly accepted our treats from eagerly outstretched hands. Her soft lips made us smile when they tickled our palms as she took the grass from our opened hands. She never nipped us. By this time the iceman would be standing at the back of the wagon and we hastily formed a line to receive our cool summer treat. A piece of ice, flaked with sawdust, that had to be brushed off, but not too closely.

Now a piece of ice may not sound like a big deal to today's youngsters but to us it tasted sweeter than any popsicle or ice cream cone. While you sucked on these bits of coolness some always dripped down your tanned torso. These icy rivulets of water left small white lines on your dusty belly. This always made you grin and shiver at the same time. The best part was you didn't have to save your allowance for a week to buy it.

Today was my turn to be first. This meant I got the biggest piece of ice. I don't know how he did it, but the iceman always knew who should be first, so he kept us honest. After handing out the first piece of ice he made sure all the smaller children came next. No shy little girl or boy was going to leave his wagon without a piece of cool ice to make them smile.

We then stood around sucking our little bit of heaven and watch this muscular man perform his wizardry with an ice pick. It was a sight to behold. He could carve a 100 pound block of ice into smaller, perfectly square blocks within minutes. Grasping his ice pick firmly in his strong hands he began an up-and-down motion that was so rapid his arm looked like a blur. As the chips flew in all directions we moved closer so they would fall on our shirtless, warm skin with all their coolness. These small, symmetrical blocks always fit perfectly into your icebox.

The iceman always wore a warm plaid shirt, even in the summer. Strapped to his shoulder was a large piece of leather. Its function was to provide a platform for the ice to rest upon after he had swung it effortlessly to his shoulder with a pair of large ice tongs. These tongs reminded me of an extra pair of arms ending in sharp points instead of hands and fingers. By this time, Mom stood on the front porch, brought outside by our laughing commotion. Because it was Wednesday she had just cleaned out the icebox in preparation for fresh ice. Moms just don't seem to forget about things like this. She then led the iceman inside with all of us following closely in his long strides. We wanted to see if the block of ice he had fashioned with his pick would really fit in the icebox. It always did, just like a piece in a large jigsaw puzzle.

We then hurried back outside so we could get a second piece of ice before Dolly grew impatient to get to her next stop. This second piece was usually followed by a gentle pat on our heads from the massive hands of this kindly man.

Once again, they started down the street toward another neighborhood stop, where Dolly knew another group of children would be waiting. Their hands would also be full of grass to satisfy her endless appetite.

Yes, even today I call our refrigerator an icebox. This confuses my grandchildren because they have no idea what I'm talking about. They just chalk it up to grandpa wisdom. Someday, as we're having a grandfather,-grandchild talk, I'll tell them the story of the iceman and Dolly.

Changing times first replaced Dolly with a truck that could carry twice as much ice as she could but certainly didn't know how to stop at a customer's familiar house without a command. Next, it wasn't long before the iceman himself was replaced by a newfangled thing called a refrigerator. Moms everywhere were excited about this new modern kitchen convenience. But we children knew we had lost two very dear friends as well as our cool treats. The stoic ice cubes that were stored in the top of the refrigerator never tasted as good as a piece of ice sprinkled with sawdust that had to be brushed off, but not too carefully.

Occasionally, even today as I take ice cubes from the refrigerator, I remember this friendly man who had arms as big as stumps, and his horse Dolly. They're gone, but not forgotten, by me or the rest of the gang that sat on the curb in the hot summer sun, waiting patiently for them to come into view.

Shaking my head, I return to reality and begin to pencil in her requested changes. By this time my wife is at my side, smiling, and says, "You do such great work, no wonder I married you". I think to myself, "That makes two of us."

The smile on her face makes it all worthwhile.

MY FRIENDLY ALARM CLOCK

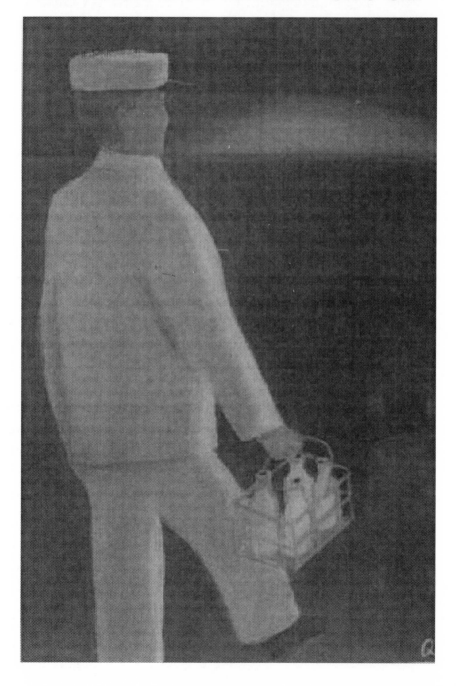

Today's supermarkets have changed the way the American way of shopping for food, not all for the better in my opinion. One of the great pleasures of my growing up was listening for the milkman early in the morning. As this kindly man in his sparkling white uniform approached our front porch, the bottles in his carrying container clinked melodically. It was a most pleasant sound, much more soothing than an alarm clock.

One morning he caught me peeking out through the curtains of my second floor bedroom window. He smiled up at me and waved, as he turned and started back to his freshly washed truck. He was whistling as usual. From then on I'm sure he looked up every morning to see if I was there.

In the summertime this type of awaking was eagerly anticipated. Can you say this about one of those noisy, sleep-robbing, mechanical, laminated monsters called an alarm clock? Certainly no one is having bright cheery thoughts while reaching over to still its unwelcome voice.

As the milkman woke me at five thirty on a summer morning, the birds chirped with wild abandon. The-early-morning fresh air, scented with the sweet smell of blooming flowers in spring and summer, gently rustled the curtains as it drifted in my window. Its coolness felt good on my warm skin. Now I could start my day. Who wants to sleep in when you have the whole day ahead of you? This man who delivered our milk would also come around during the day to sell Mother all the extras produced by the dairy. My Father warned Mother not to buy any, but she only smiled. After all, she knew how much he enjoyed the extra treats.

On cold winter mornings, when my sleep was disturbed by his tinkling steps, I smiled. I knew I could sleep for another hour before I had to get up. It was dark and no thought of arising early crossed my mind.

I guess you could call the milkman my snooze alarm during the winter months. This extra hour allowed me the pleasure of having my Dad get up and go to the basement to build a roaring fire in the furnace. As soon as Dad opened the basement door my dog, Spud, so named because he was round and the color of a potato, bolted for my bedroom, and with wagging tail and wet tongue he snuggled down in my soft sheet blankets. I hoped my bedroom floor would be warm by the time I had to put my feet on it. While I lay in bed, I wondered if it was cold enough to freeze the milk and allow it to expand, pushing the milk and cream upward out of the bottle. These castle-like creations often had the bottle caps sitting on top of the frozen milk protruding from the bottle. In my imagination the bottles reminded me of soldiers in formation with helmets on their heads. We could gauge how cold it was by how high the frozen milk protruded above the bottle, looking like the mercury in a thermometer. I once caught our cat enjoying a special treat as she stood on her hind legs and licked the frozen cream.

Too bad today's children will never be able to snuggle down in their blankets on a cold winter morning and wonder if the milk on the porch will freeze. They will sleep in on bright, sunny summer mornings and miss the sunrise. The birds will be busy socializing with their chirping and the sleepyheads will never hear their songs, all because they have no friendly alarm clock.

Sometimes as I lay in bed in the morning, listening to my friendly alarm, I pondered about a career as a milkman. This field didn't rate as high as a policeman or fireman but it was close to the top. I could only imagine how exciting it must have been in the early years when the milkman had a horse pulling his wagon. This little side benefit would have rated high on my list.

They called it a door-to-door service, but I call it a bit of Americana that unfortunately has all but disappeared. Believe me, the dairy case in the supermarket will stir no fond memories in my children or grandchildren. To them it's only a shiny, sterile piece of machinery where the milk for their cereal is stored.

Certainly the frost inside that dairy case will never generate the warmth I felt as our milkman looked up at me, smiled and waved.

A GRANDPA'S GOOD OLD DAYS

It was late one evening when my seven-year-old grandson Joshua crawled onto my lap as I read the paper. I was sure he wanted me to read to him before he went to bed, something we always did when he stayed overnight. I asked him, "What do you want to read tonight?" He surprised me when he said, "I just want you to tell me, what were the *good old days*, Grandpa?" "That's easy," I said.

They were your first day of school. When you fully realized you had a mind of your own and were expected to use it. You found out quickly Mom and Dad wouldn't be around with their protective tenderness.

You learn you don't always win at marbles and many other games in life. Through the tears, your skinned knees, and bruised ego, these now became the first of your *good old days*. To quote the poet Robert Frost, "But you have promises to keep and miles to go before you sleep." Josh smiled at that, not really knowing what to make of my bit of poetry, but he will someday.

They were the days when you were chosen first for the neighborhood team of afternoon softball or football. School summer vacations spent at the ol' swimming hole. Fishing trips with Dad, where every fish was a keeper and the big one didn't get away. Saturday matinees and the time spent playing with your dog Spud were also part of your *good old days* during this period of your life. Josh said, "Yeah, I like to play with Ebony, my dog, and fish too."

Occasionally Dad, with his commanding voice and tall stature made veiled threats. "If you don't get that lawn mowed there won't be any allowance this week." This warning always brought about long sessions with our push reel type mower. As much as I begged he would have none of those new rotary self-propelled mowers. He used to say, "Why should I get one of those mechanical mowers when I already have a mower powered by a one half-horse power Nelson?" Oh, for those *good old days*. Josh smiled and said, "I know the feeling. I have to mow the yard also, Grandpa."

"Would you like me to go on, Josh?" "Yes," he answered in his childlike voice, "don't stop now." "Ok," I said.

You took your shirt and shoes off around the middle of June and seldom had them on again until school started in September. Nobody ever heard of sunscreen. Wednesday afternoon you didn't play golf like many professional people. You waited on the curb with your friends for the iceman and his horse Dolly. This kindly man, whose arms looked like stumps, made muscular from delivering ice, was quick to pass out samples of his product. While you sucked on these bits of coolness some always melted and dripped down your tanned torso. These icy rivulets of water, leaving small white lines on your bare, dusty belly, made you smile and shiver at the same time. Josh squirmed a little as he pulled up his shirt to check his belly.

They were your first date, first kiss, and first love. When the only concern you had was the next day's algebra exam. Yeah, right, as if schoolwork was a priority in your young life! Your biggest problem was wondering if that cute member of the opposite sex would call you that night. Or, heaven forbid, if your new clothes didn't correspond to the latest fad. Hopefully, Dad would let you use his car for Saturday night. When you got in trouble at school you also got in trouble at home. Yes, believe it or not, these were the *good old days*.

Your first date with that cute girl from English class was also one of your *good old days*. Josh put his hand to his head and frowned a little at this statement. Just like any normal seven-year-old boy, remember? Then came a magical moment when your hand reached out for hers in the darkness of the theater. You were amazed at its softness. Certainly not rough like yours. When her hand responded with a gentle squeeze you were not prepared for the strange new warm sensation that flowed between you both. Yes, this date and those exciting first-time emotions that awoke within you will definitely become one of your *good old days*. It was easy to continue, as Josh kept repeating, "Grandpa, please go on."

All the school dances, wiener roasts, sporting events and summer vacations at the lakes must also be mentioned. The most fun of all was the carefree feeling without being pretentious. Mom used to say, "Your school years are the best years of your life." This was hard to believe when you were faced with one adolescent crisis after another.

You matured and mellowed during your *good old days* of college. Choosing a lifelong career and a mate for life. Oh well, in this day and age, one out of two ain't bad. Josh nodded and agreed with this even though he wasn't sure just what I meant.

They were your army days when all you remember are the good times spent with your buddies on weekend passes. I knew this would interest Josh. He always liked to hear about my army days. Seems like all he ever wore were some camouflaged army pants his Grandma had bought him for Christmas and an old army fatigue hat I had given him.

The furloughs spent with your best girl before leaving for an extended period of time. Seems like the two of you were always trying to squeeze a lifetime into a few short weeks of togetherness. The quiet time just before your departure when you both pledged your love through tears. The feeling of loving someone and being loved in return is hard to describe. It becomes and remains a driving force throughout your life. Hard to believe these days of uncertainty would become part of your *good old days*, but they did.

Marriages lasted because men tempered on the battlefield accepted responsibility for themselves and the others around them. Women left at home, with their inner strength, accepted separation and loneliness. Even though separated by thousands of miles, couples remained as one.

"Drug problems were almost nonexistent," I continued. A natural high was attained by working to achieve victory and the reformation of your family. A plant or chemical substance was not necessary. These were the days that tried men's souls and they will be remembered as trying *good old days*. Hopefully I wasn't beyond Josh at this point, I thought.

Then I noticed Josh's head was beginning to nod as he snuggled against my shoulder. I knew he was getting sleepy and I stopped once more only to hear him murmur in a soft voice, "Please go on, Grandpa."

They were the return to civilian life and the beginning of your career and family. Like they used to say, all you wanted to do was "get crackin'," I continued.

Your firstborn certainly qualifies as a major feature in your memories of the *good old days*. Who can forget that tiny bundle of responsibility as it nestled in your arms smiling and cooing? You felt sure their first word, first sentence, and first step would never come but of course they did. Your *good old days* now encompassed all the dreams you would have for this child.

The trials you will face raising that child never enter your mind. Josh murmured something like, "I have dreams too, Grandpa. I want to be a soldier." This was no surprise to me.

Good old days were part of your rise up the ladder in your career field, long before the word *downsizing* had become a very active verb in the vocabulary of corporate America. Those *good old days* were so busy you often forgot to eat. Now you remember to eat but wish you hadn't as you gaze wistfully into your full-length mirror. Josh said, "Grandpa, you're not fat." I must remember to give him a treat later, I thought.

All family gatherings, such as births, christenings, birthdays, graduations, Christmases, Fourty of July's and anniversaries all become part of your *good old days*. Your first grandchild comes along and you start the cycle once again. For they now are part of your *good old days*. Josh, at this point, woke up enough to ask, "Are we going to have a party, Grandpa?" "Yes, and you will be the guest of honor," I said. He smiled at that statement and closed his eyes.

Everyone remembers and speaks of their very own *good old days*. Many will be the same as yours. Some may differ just slightly. If I left out anything from your definition of *good old days*, I'm sorry. It is certainly possible, because as one accumulates all those *good old days* one's memory just might—I said "just might"—get a little shorter. One thing for sure, most will depict the same milestones and periods of time in each individual's life. Sleepyhead Josh was fading fast.

So don't look perplexed, Josh, when someone asks, "What are the *good old days*?" Your explanation can be simple when you stop and think about it. Every day of your life eventually becomes part of your fond memories of the *good old days*. Today, tomorrow, next week and next year should and can be the best *good old days* of the rest of your life. They can be if you will just let them. Remember, it's up to you.

I might have well saved my breath by this time for Josh was sound asleep. I gently picked him up and took him to our guest room. I stood for a moment looking down at his tousled blond hair and tiny sleeping form with a warm feeling and a smile on my face. Turning out the light, I thought to myself, "Thanks Josh, this is certainly one of my best good old days. Good night and sleep tight."

MAGIC WORDS

A heavy snowstorm was developing as I sat in my car at a major intersection. I wondered if the snow would ever stop. Then a large van pulled up across the intersection from me. All of a sudden a young girl jumped out of the passenger side on a dead run. She had a smile on her face as big as the snowy outdoors. She scurried around the van to replace, I assumed, her father. He had just gotten out on the driver's side and was headed around the van to the passenger side. He had undoubtedly uttered those magic words, "Would you like to drive?" to his daughter. Yes, these are truly magic words to the ears of any young person learning how to drive.

I passed them as we both pulled out and saw who I'm sure were Mom and younger sister, in the back seat of the van. Sister had pulled a newspaper up in front of her face as if for protection, and was probably saying something like, "Dad, you can't let her drive in this snow with us in the car, it's dangerous." Mom probably retorted with "Hush dear, she has to start sometime. She has had safe driving at school." As if this was going to make sister feel more secure and lessen her envy.

Taking a final glance at the van in my rear view mirror I watched the van disappear in the distance. The young girl looked like a tiny munchkin behind the wheel of such a large vehicle.

It was then I remembered those magic words, "Would you like to get in my lap and steer, son?" So began my odyssey of learning how to drive. Most of us have gone through it in some form or another.

I was eight or nine when Dad spoke these magic words to me as we drove home from the store in the Hudson. He might as well have asked me if I wanted some chocolate cake and ice cream. The answer would have been the same. A resounding "yes." Smiling, I climbed up in his lap and steered the final two blocks home.

When we got out of the car Dad said, "Don't tell your mother, son. She wouldn't understand." He didn't have to tell me not to tell my two irritating sisters—that was a given. I agreed with a nod. I wouldn't be lying, just not volunteering any information. Sounded perfectly reasonable to me. You learn these lessons when you are a young boy with two sisters and an inquiring, inquisitive mother. I knew Dad fully understood my reasoning.

After occasional turns at the steering wheel through the years, I eventually advanced to shifting gears. This was accomplished sitting next to Dad and shifting when he put in the clutch, followed by the word, "Shift," in a gruff voice. I learned quickly to shift with accuracy for a reason. Grinding gears always brought a scowl to Dad's face and the end of my lesson for the day. I certainly didn't want this to happen.

These learning lessons ceased as I got older and couldn't sit in his lap anymore. Besides, by this time I was dreaming of those magic words myself, "Would you like to drive, Jimmy?" Knowing at this stage in my life we were talking the real thing—Solo. I was sure age sixteen would never come because that was the age you had to be to get a driver's license in my state.

There is a lot to be said for the old expression, "Sweet sixteen and never been kissed." A girl's first kiss can be a major milestone in her life as well as a boy's. But this is nothing compared to the boy's first driver's license and solo trip behind the wheel of the family car. Fifty years ago a driver's license meant freedom never before experienced by a youngster. Of course, this newfound freedom also meant responsible actions.

A driver's license was important to the female gender also although not in the same manner. After all, it would have been highly unusual back in the '50s to see a young girl pick up a date in the family Hudson. This is not true today. It happens all the time, except it's not in a Hudson. It's probably a Honda. Too bad, the Hudson became a shrine.

I'm sure there isn't a male alive who doesn't remember the day he passed the driving test. If he were dating a particular girl, she wouldn't forget either. Music over the car radio would sound so much sweeter than the phonograph or radio in the front room. It feels so good not to be under Mom and Dad's watchful eye.

A harvest moon shines much brighter and more meaningfully through the windshield of a parked car. You didn't even notice the dirty windshield from your cozy, strategic viewing point.

Dances and wiener roasts in the country were also possible. Most of them in the past had been beyond the end of the bus line. Now the only line you had to worry about was the lines of responsibility. Curfews were usually kept, for no boy wanted to lose access to the family car. He could no longer use the excuse the bus was late or didn't come at all. In an occasional extreme emergency he could fall back on a flat tire or I *ran out of gas*. But not too often. Dads and Moms were young once, too.

If you have a young boy or girl in your family, rest assured these words still hold the same magic for them as they did for you— "Would you like to drive?"

RESERVED SEAT

My grandfather's rocking chair was made of oak. It was straight-backed without arms and complete with a scruffy brown leather seat. On one side, where the seat met the back, it was held together with bailing wire. This chair enjoyed a special place of honor in my grandfather and grandmother's home, a stately house with pillars on the porch and ivy stretching across the front.

The chair sat in their living room close to a large black pot-bellied wood-burning heating stove. No one sat in this chair but Grandpa. It was his and his alone. Sort of like a throne, humble in its simplicity, in honor of all the labor he had performed throughout his life, first as a farmer, then as a hard rock miner and ending up digging ditches for the local gas company. All the jobs he ever had in his seventy-eight years were associated with Mother Earth and a pick and shovel. Yet he always provided food, clothing, and shelter for his wife and twelve children without complaint, often being away at the mines for months at a time. He never owned a car and had little except the simple pleasures of life, and the love and respect of his family.

Grandpa worked the mines in the Wallace Kellogg area. Two of these mines were the Starr and Galenia mines. It was a physically demanding job and a rough place to live. Grandpa and Grandma and their twelve children lived in an extremely narrow canyon near the mines where Grandpa worked. The canyon was so narrow that when the daily train came into town, the stores along the main street had to pull up their store awnings. Years later I would see pictures and read stories about Burke Canyon in history books.

Mom said her job as a small girl was simple. When Grandpa got home from the mine all tired and dirty, she was given 50¢ and sent to the corner saloon to get him a tin bucket of cold beer. It was a nice walk and if she got home without spilling too much of the golden liquid, she got to keep the change. Mom said she never ran. She ended her story with, "Before the train went back down the canyon, Grandma would have to bring in the wash from the line, so it wouldn't be carried off when the train went by."

Another favorite story of mine was about the time Grandpa was in a mine cave-in. The cave-in broke his leg, which ended up in a cast. Grandma said Grandpa got so mad when he had to stay home from work that he took a hammer and broke off the cast so he could get back to work. Grandpa would smile, saying, "I only did it because I wanted a cold bucket of beer after a hard day's work." Grandma told him to hush, there were grandkids listening.

I never ceased to wonder at the steel nerves of this man. The soft canvas hat he had worn in the mines would have offered him no protection in case of falling rock. The small carbide lantern attached on its front would have produced very little light in the damp, dark tunnels in which he worked. These mementos and others became my playthings while I was growing up, as well as part of my fond memories of this man.

I remember so vividly as a child, watching him rocking in his chair at the end of the day, the only time he had to sit in it. In the evening, the twilight shadows slowly crept across the living room's linoleum-covered floor eventually creating only a silhouette of this kindly man, while the flames inside the woodstove, reflecting through its tiny window, danced upon his weathered features. The crackling and popping of burning tamarack only added to his mystique as he slowly rocked back and forth, causing the gold nugget on his watch fob to glisten in the flickering firelight.

I always waited with anticipation for that slight squeak I knew would come from the rocker's wired joint as he completed his backward motion. In my mind, it added character to his melodic rocking, wump-wump-squeak.

He never sat in his chair for long before Susie, his German shorthaired pointer, who never pointed at anything except her dog dish, would be at his side. She knew it was only a matter of time before his hand reached out and find her head with his soft touch. This dog, whom he often referred to as "that old pot hound" always looked up at him with adoration and wagging tail, knowing full well she would be sleeping by his bed that night.

The only time his chair was moved was on Saturday night. He would take it to the front room and set it next to a small table radio, encased in a beautiful maple cabinet. There he rocked and laughed incessantly at the satirical humor of two of America's favorite comedy giants, Amos and Andy. I believe today's counterpart could best be described in the humor of characters in the comic strip Doonesbury. The rest of the family ended up retreating to the living room so they wouldn't have to hear him say in his gruffest voice, "Shush now, I'm trying to listen."

Before I was tall enough to reach the top of their back gate I would stand there looking through the wire, watching for him to come home from work. I could see him coming blocks away, walking briskly, his worn, shiny lunchbox under his arm. I eagerly awaited his arrival since we had this little game we always played. I knew he had saved his dessert from lunch for me, and as he came through the gate, I asked, "Did you save anything for me?" He'd grin, look down at my outstretched arms and hand me the lunchbox saying, "I don't know. You will have to look inside." I opened the lid slowly, knowing full well the dessert would be there and it always was. I learned later in life that Grandma packed two desserts in his lunch when I visited. So he wouldn't go without.

The deer-hunting trip that sticks in my mind the most was a four-day affair with Dad, Grandpa, two uncles, and me. Grandpa was in charge of bringing all the food and planning the meals. Our first night at camp he placed a big plate of bread and beans before us. The next morning at breakfast we also had beans and bread. By this time we were all wondering what he would provide for dinner that night. Sure enough, it was beans and bread. Finally, my Dad asked, "Are beans and bread all we're going to get on this four-day hunt?" Grandpa looked at him sternly and said, "We didn't come up here to eat. We came us here to hunt." Nothing more was said.

In the summer he always wore a full-brimmed straw hat, that came to a pointy peak on top of his head. The green eyeshade sewn in front of the brim cast a soft green hue over his eyes giving him a grandfather's gentle look as we toiled together in his small garden, while Susie lay nearby dozing in the sun on a pile of warm, soft dirt.

Most of all, I'm fortunate to have the memory of Grandpa gently rocking in his chair with Susie at his side. He was gruff, yet gentle, and in his rocker, represented so much more to me than just a grandpa. He stood for hard work and sacrifice for his family, not to mention the great role model he presented to all of us. These thoughts are always accompanied by a warm feeling whenever I see an old, straight-backed, armless rocker with a brown scruffy seat. I really hope some day to find one with baling wire holding one of its back joints together. It will happen.

We didn't have many years together—he left us when I was twelve—but all of them were packed with adventure and learning. We went on hunting and fishing trips, and took long walks and had long talks. Most were filled with grandfatherly wisdom and advice. It's unfortunate so many children grow up today without a grandfather's strong influence.

Yes, I always puff up a little with pride as I remember the man I have always striven to be like. My namesake, Grandpa Jim.

THE CLASS OF '50
(A GENTLER TIME)

The study hall was so quiet you could hear a cat walk, if there had been a cat walking. All of a sudden a loud voice shattered the silence, "Are you going to the senior prom, Jim?" The voice seemed to echo across the room.

I crunched down in my seat hoping no one knew who Jim was and thought to myself, "Some friend you are, Bill. Thanks a lot. I'll talk to you later."

With this thought in mind I slunk out of study hall and headed for home as the last bell had just rung. While walking home I thought, "What's the big deal? It's just the senior prom. I'll go if I want to."

As was my habit, I arrived home and strolled into the kitchen for a peanut butter and jelly sandwich. Mom was busy preparing dinner. "I hope we have pork chops tonight," I thought to myself. Then right out of the blue, like most parents do, she hit me with the Big One.

"You haven't mentioned your senior prom, Jimmy. You are going, aren't you?"

"What's all the fuss?" I said. "I really haven't given it much thought." What a fib that was, when in reality I had given it a lot of thought. After this statement I retreated to the living room to savor my sandwich.

Dad had just got home from work and was reading the Chronicle, our evening newspaper, something he did every night. As I slouched down on the sofa I turned on the radio—no TV in those days. Dad looked up over the paper, as most Dads do, and said, "Not too loud, Jimmy, I'm trying to concentrate on the paper. Oh, and by the way, I haven't heard you mention your senior prom." I'd had it. I grunted something unintelligible and headed for my room, peanut butter and jelly sandwich in hand.

Lying on my bed in the privacy of my room, I stared at the ceiling and began to run the visions and names of several girls I knew through my mind. Joy, a cute, perky blonde with blue eyes that liked to laugh. Phyllis, a dark-haired cheerleader, cute as a button, "Nah, she wouldn't go with me," I thought, "Besides she is going out with a football player, much bigger than me." "Donna, a real sweet, tiny thing from my math class might be nice," I continued to think. "No way," the answer came back. "She is smarter than me."

The next thing I knew Mom was at my bedroom door knocking, "Dinner is ready, Jimmy. We're having pork chops." Once more, like moms everywhere, she had read my mind.

As prom night drew closer I still hadn't made up my mind who to ask. It wasn't because I knew so many girls; it was that I really wanted this to be a real special night. After all, this was supposed to be a night to remember for the rest of your life.

It had been an agonizing two weeks since Bill had yelled across the study hall asking if I had a date for the senior prom when I finally decided. I would ask Gloria. What a relief. Now I knew who I was going to ask but I still didn't know if she would accept. "I'll cross that bridge when I come to it," I thought.

Gloria was a sophomore and I was a senior but I didn't feel this would be a hurdle. She had always shown an interest in me, in a quiet sort of way. She had long dark hair and a smile that would almost blind you. She sort of floated when she walked and her infectious laugh always made you feel warm inside. Yes, Gloria would be the one.

The next day after this major decision, I happened upon Gloria in the hustle and bustle of changing classes. I spotted her walking thirty feet in front of me in the noisy crowd, dark long hair in a sea of bobbing heads. Gathering up all my courage, I hurried to catch up with her, recalling the speech I had practiced the night before.

I was soon at her side and softly touched her arm. She slowed, looked up at me, smiled, and said, "Hi Jim, where are you headed?" "Oh just to class, how about you?" I said. "Same for me," she replied. I knew this was my chance, it wouldn't give her much time to think about it. "Gloria," I said hesitantly, "Would you like to go to the senior prom with me?" Without hesitation she said, "I didn't think you would ever ask. Of course I will, Jim!" Dumb old me, the grapevine had done its job well. I'm sure it still does. She knew I was going to ask her before I knew myself. Yes, girls, guys go through the same emotions as you do in this thing they call the dating game.

I think my Mom was as excited as I was on the big night. I also got calls from Grandma, Auntie Irene, and my married sister in another state. Plus a couple of older cousins all telling me what to do and say. I had no idea the preparation one had to go through for the big night; corsage, suit pressed—no one had a tux or the money to rent one—new shirt and tie, shined shoes, et cetera. I also had to work extra hard around the house for spending money.

The big question was—would Dad let me use the Hudson? Three days before the dance, after I had turned down a couple of rides with friends, I approached Dad. He was all relaxed after dinner listening to the radio. As I stood next to him he looked up and said, "The big dance is Saturday, isn't it, Jimmy?" Surprised that he remembered, I said, "Yes," to which he replied, "I want you home by 1 AM and if you get the Hudson dirty you have to wash it on Sunday." "You bet," I hollered as I ran out of the room to call Gloria. We would be going to the prom in the Hudson! It was good to be alive.

Gloria looked fabulous when I picked her up and that's much better than cool. I went through the necessary ritual of meeting her folks before we left and they certainly seemed pleasant enough. You must remember I had never met them, as this would be our first date. Her Dad's voice followed us out the door, "Take good care of my little girl, Jim, and have her home at a reasonable hour."

We made small talk, as the radio played softly in the darkness of the car on the way to the dance. I distinctly remember hearing some Glen Miller, Frank Sinatra, and Les Paul and Mary Ford singing the "Tennessee Waltz." I could hardly wait to get there, since I loved to dance. I had watched Gloria at the school dances and I knew she liked to dance also. No valet parking in these times. We parked blocks away because the spaces around the hotel were all filled.

It was just like I imagined it would be when we walked into the ballroom and the music was playing. Balloons were everywhere and all the tables had been set with white linen tablecloths and fresh flowers. Our school colors woven into small pom poms were placed in front of each chair. The piece de resistance was the large flickering candle bowl in the center of the table. Yes, I still remember after all these years.

Between dances, both Gloria and I visited with friends and became somewhat acquainted. She was just like I imagined she would be. Funny, talkative, and full of laughter and besides all of this she was a good dancer.

It seemed like we had just got there when the band started playing Good Night Irene.

"They must be kidding, it's not midnight yet," I thought. I looked down at Gloria while we danced and thought, "Sure enough it must be midnight." She had her eyes half-closed and she looked sleepy in a sultry kind of way. Although I really wasn't even sure what sultry meant. "It's time to go, Gloria." I said. She replied, "I know, darn it. I could dance all night."

While we drove home in the Hudson, I again heard the "Tennessee Waltz," only this time it was by Patti Page. Yes, it was a fitting ending to a perfect evening.

When we got to Gloria's house the porch light was on and also a light just inside the door. I really didn't expect all the light but with surging male courage, I took her in my arms and gave her a warm goodnight kiss. She responded in kind and I knew then she also had enjoyed the evening. As I bid her goodnight and started down the walk toward the Hudson I thought, "Yes, this will be a night to remember."

Fifty years have passed since this night and yes they are right. You never forget your senior prom, even when you are a grandparent. I hope Gloria hasn't forgotten either.

BLUE SUEDES

It was a shimmering hot, sunny Saturday morning in June 1956 and all was right in my young world. I was headed downtown to Les Critzer's Men's Shoe Store—our town's favorite men's shoe store for young and old alike. When you opened the door to this fine haberdashery you were always met with the smell of newly polished leather. It's hard to describe this pleasant odor but it always tickled my nose and caused me to smile.

Mr. Critzer met me at the door with a cheery "Hello, young man. What can I do for you today?" Without hesitation I said, "I want to see some blue suede shoes and white bucks." He made an about-face that would make a drill sergeant proud and said in a commanding voice, "Follow me." For just a moment I thought I was in the army.

Life-size posters of celebrities wearing different shoe styles adorned the walls. They caught my attention as I followed Mr. Critzer back to the shoe showroom. It seemed like their eyes followed me stride for stride. The two standouts were Elvis Presley and Pat Boone. Elvis was attired in a pair of casual blue suede shoes. They seemed so much like him, along with his white shirt open to the center of his chest and white flared pants held up with a wide white belt. He looked like he could shake, rattle, and roll right off the wall. His right hand was limply thrust into the waistband of his pants. They were held up, in my mind's eye, with what else but a narrow blue suede belt. I also hoped to buy one of these fashion statements very soon, to match my blue suede shoes of course.

The Pat Boone poster with him in his white bucks was almost as impressive. His hair was shorter than Elvis's and the demeanor of his pose more mature but without a doubt your eyes remained transfixed on his white bucks.

A poster of a slouching James Dean, legs crossed at the ankles, leaning against a Model A Coup Classic street rod, with a cigarette dangling from his mouth, should have completed the scene. But alas, no James Dean. "He wasn't known for his shoes or clothes," I reflected, "more for his doleful eyes and soft voice."

I listened to Mr. Critzer's sales pitch; we always called our elders Mister in those days. Now that I have reached senior status, youngsters seldom use *Mister* anymore but that's ok, I don't feel like a senior either.

He put my foot up on his shoe stool and droned, "Blue suedes and white bucks are the latest fashion. They will wear like iron and you will look good in them." As a young man with a $20 bill, from my first summer paycheck, in the pocket of my Levi's (aka James Dean), I was ready to buy. I didn't need a sales pitch. I knew what I wanted, and besides, the male gender is not blessed with the love-to-shop gene.

After measuring my foot, Mr. Critzer disappeared behind his wall of boxed shoes and reappeared almost instantly. Smiling, he said, "I have just one pair of blue suedes in size seven, but you're in luck. I have several of your size in white bucks." This certainly wouldn't make it easier for me to make a choice. Should I take the single pair of blue suedes or choose from the large selection of white bucks?

While I was contemplating this major decision in my life, Mr. Critzer rested himself once more on the shoe stool, placing my right foot on the slanted front.

As he almost lovingly placed the blue suede shoe on my right foot, I thought, "All I need now are some white pants with a wide white belt and white shirt open exposing my chest, and some Brylcream—look out girls, here I come."

I was daydreaming about how great I would look in the blue suedes when he quickly placed a white buck shoe on my left foot. I was brought back to awareness when he jerked my foot sharply while tying it tightly with a checkered shoelace. "Wow," I thought, "colored shoelaces and everything." *Look out, Pat Boone, I can't sing but I can dance and Saturday night is coming.*

I can't tell you the turmoil I went through. What's it going to be, white bucks or blue suedes—blue suedes or white bucks? As I grasped the $20 bill in my tight Levi pocket. I knew it had to be one or the other, since I didn't have enough money for both pairs. I knew the decision had to be quick because another customer had just walked into Mr. Critzer's fine haberdashery.

I just knew this customer was after blue suede shoes and he certainly looked like he could wear a size seven. Mr. Critzer excused himself and said he would be right back and for me to think about it while he greeted his new customer. "What's it going to be, blue suedes or white bucks?" I pondered.

Mr. Critzer returned much too quickly and said "Young man, I can see you like both the blue suede and thewhite buck shoes. Tell you what, why don't you buy the blue suedes and put the white bucks on layaway?"

It was so simple. "Why didn't I think of that? Must be because males just don't have that love-to-shop gene," I thought to myself.

As we completed our transaction, I thanked Mr. Critzer and said I would return next payday to pick up my white bucks.

With a parting handshake I headed for the door and walked outside into the sunshine on that glorious Saturday afternoon. Wearing my new blue suedes I felt on top of the world. I then remembered there was a Saturday night dance—lookout girls, I can't sing but I sure can dance.

SUSIE GETS THE BIRD

Susie was the first bird dog I ever hunted behind. She was a German short haired pointer and the proud pet of my grandfather. Like the nursery rhyme, wherever Grandpa went, Susie was sure to go. During the day this pair most often could be found in Grandpa's workshop. In the growing season they were in the garden, Grandpa weeding and Susie stretched out on the soft tilled earth sunning herself. She was always careful never to lie on anything growin —yeah right.

In the evening Grandpa would sit in his armless straight-back rocker. Susie moved closer to his side as he rocked, knowing full well his hand would soon find her head with his soft touch. Wump —stroke, wump—stroke, wump—stroke.

It was never long before Grandpa was dozing and Susie fell asleep standing up. On more than one occasion she would fall over and the rest of the family had a heartfelt laugh. This always awoke Grandpa with a start and a frown in our direction.

Grandpa was quite proud of Susie's so-called hunting prowess. He used to tell me in all seriousness that she was so close to being overtrained he had to let her rest for a whole year. With the gullibility of a doting eight-year-old grandson, I believed everything my Grandpa said. I found out later that Grandpa actually believed it himself. The big day finally arrived. At age eight I was going on my first pheasant hunt with Grandpa, Susie and Dad.

I never slept the night before, as I kept dreaming of Susie racing across a field with a pheasant in her mouth headed in my direction. It was a beautiful sight. Susie, her liver and white coat flashing in the sun, bounding through the stubble—head and tail up and her eyes flashing in pure joy. There was only one problem. I wasn't carrying a gun, since I was too young, so I couldn't have shot it. It didn't matter because I woke up at this time to Dad's voice, "It's 5 A.M. Jimmy, time to get up." I jumped out of bed at the sound of his soft voice. He didn't want to wake the rest of the family.

We'd planned this trip for months. I wouldn't be carrying a gun; that would come at age twelve, after a couple of years of learning about firearm safety and the animals and birds I'd be hunting. But it would be my first pheasant hunt nonetheless.

There was only one individual more excited than I was and that was Susie as we all climbed into the station wagon. She barely sat still on the 100-mile-plus car ride to what Dad called "pheasant heaven." I thought this was a great name and just knew every pheasant we shot would end up in heaven. Just like the name implied. I learned later Dad was referring to this bit of land as heaven for the hunters, not the birds. I still believe my description was more accurate —especially to an eight-year-old boy.

As we drove along I wondered why Dad kept saying to Grandpa—Grandpa's name was Jim also—"Jim, I sure hope that well-trained dog of yours hunts well today. We are going a long way and I want Jimmy to have a rewarding and memorable hunt." Grandpa just smiled and said, "Don't worry, I have got this dog trained to a fine edge." I squirmed with pleasure and envisioned ol' Susie on a picture-perfect point. A beautifully bright, multicolored pheasant would burst skyward from beneath our feet on Dad's command, "Flush, Susie, flush." Grandpa would be off to the side smiling. I would be softly saying, "Good girl, Susie, good girl. Get the bird, get the bird."

It seemed forever but we finally arrived at pheasant heaven. We were in rolling hills and fresh-cut stubble containing a few brushy eyebrows the farmer couldn't cultivate. Typical pheasant country in any hunter's book.

As the car came to a stop my excitement continued to escalate. Susie was as excited as I was. I could tell because she was jumping up and down in the back seat, drooling, whining and she even passed a little gas. Dad turned toward the back seat and said, "That's enough of that, ol' girl, or you won't come again." Grandpa just smiled, I said "Phew."

We parked the car and began to lay plans. Dad, like an officer in charge of troops began to map out a plan of attack. "Jim," he said to Grandpa, "You go up the south end of that eyebrow with Susie and Jimmy, and I will come in from the north. Hopefully if there are any birds in there we will run them toward each other." Grandpa nodded in agreement and we all started to gather up our gear.

I was in charge of lunch and because we would be gone for quite a while I carefully put some sandwiches in my knapsack, not forgetting a couple of dog biscuits for Susie.

With our well-laid plans we all set out with joyful enthusiasm. Susie was the first one out. In her excitement she had passed some more gas. Susie immediately began to run and bound in a zigzag fashion through the stubble. Grandpa said with pride in his voice, "What did I tell you, the ol' girl is razor sharp. Get ready because we're going to see birds anytime."

His prideful words caused my stomach to tighten up with excitement. At the same time I noticed Dad gripping his shotgun just a little tighter with each step. Just like in my dream, I thought. Soon Susie will be racing toward us with a pheasant in her mouth. It will be a picture-perfect retrieve after a fantastic shot from Dad.

Then it happened. A large hawk that had been sitting in the stubble broke from cover in front of Susie. Its rapidly beating wings gained altitude with each graceful stroke.

Susie by this time was totally engrossed in this majestic bird and with head up took off in full stride after it. Dad and Grandpa broke into what sounded like an anvil chorus—"Here, Susie! Here, Susie! Come on, girl!" Susie paid them no heed. With each bound she was getting farther and farther away. The hawk was also getting higher and higher with each beat of its wings.

Dad and Grandpa by this time were filling the air with, "Here Susie, come, Susie," with a few well chosen expletives not really fit for an eight-year-old boy's ears, if you know what I mean. I didn't call because my small voice would have made no difference in this din of adult phases.

It was 9:30 A.M. when Susie and Mr. Hawk disappeared over the eyebrow on the distant horizon. Dad by this time was having a heated discussion with Grandpa about how overtrained Susie really was. Grandpa with a shrug of his shoulders simply said, "Everyone has a bad day, even bird dogs." I thought to myself this was true but not on my first pheasant hunt. I didn't need a bad day. We combed the area for hours and no Susie. Lunch came and went and no bones for Susie. We drove for miles in a circular manner, stopping and calling at all the likely places. Slouched in the back seat my only thought was, "Susie, where are you?"

About 4 P.M. we stopped for what we figured would be the last time before going home. With hoarse voices we all called in unison, "Here Susie! Here Susie!" There were no expletives, since they had been used up by Grandpa and Dad. By this time we were only pleading.

As we turned to get back in the car I spotted Susie coming over the horizon. She was coming full tilt across the plowed field and just like in my dream, ol' Susie had a pheasant in her mouth. She came bounding up to us just like she had been gone for only a few minutes and laid the pheasant at my feet.

We were all astounded. I reached down to pat her head and said "Good dog." Grandpa simply said, " Well, I guess you believe me now. I'm just going to have to let up on her training so she will let us shoot the birds instead of her running them down." Dad didn't say a word as we all climbed into the car but I noticed he was grinning to himself.

It was a long, silent ride home. Grandpa had fallen asleep and Dad was humming to himself while gripping the steering wheel tightly. I turned around momentarily and glanced back at Susie, bone tired, asleep in the back seat. She seemed to have a smile on her face and I noticed her feet and legs twitching as she dreamed. With a warm feeling, I said softly to myself, "You got the bird Susie. You got the bird."

WHATEVER HAPPENED
TO THE FRONT PORCH?

They say change is good since it produces progress. In most cases I agree. But there has been one change in modern architecture that I feel has done a real disservice to the American family. Yes, the single person must also be included. When the homebuilders of today eliminated the large, covered front porch they did more than save money—they destroyed a sacred tradition that has always been a part of Americana. The large front porch has been replaced by a concrete slab in the backyard called a patio. Now patios are nice, but they are a far cry from the front porch I knew and loved.

Our front porch extended all the way across the front of the house. It had ivy at both ends climbing up trellises. Also, one half of the front was enclosed in this plantlike covering. Best of all it came with a huge porch swing. One that would squeak pleasantly at just the right speed. Try and get one of these swings on a patio.

I could hardly wait for a summer storm. These storms meant I could go out and sit in the swing and watch them unfold. It would begin with the breeze rustling the ivy leaves. This rustling soon became a noisy crescendo as the wind picked up before the rain. I always hoped for thunder and lightning, because this heavenly display always brought about a warm, cozy feeling as I watched, feeling totally shielded and protected.

Sunday afternoon, in good weather, was always a great front porch day. Mom cooked a big Sunday dinner with all the fixings. At the end of the meal there were seldom any leftovers. After all the dishes were done and put away, the whole family retired to the front porch. This was the time of day all serious family discussions were put on hold. There was time only to enjoy each other's company in our favorite setting. Even I refused to squabble with my three irritating sisters.

The radio was placed in the center of the porch so everyone could hear it with programs like Red Skelton, Bing Crosby, Fibber McGee and Molly, Jack Benny, Fred Allen, Phil Harris and Alice Faye and, of course, Bob Hope. If I was allowed to stay up late, there would be Lux Radio Theater. I'm sure I left out someone's favorite program, but when you are a young boy, you only remember the one that made you laugh.

Sunday was a day of great entertainment on the front porch. Occasionally the neighborhood policeman walking his beat strolled by. He'd twirl his nightstick on its leather thong. I never did understand how this truly remarkable maneuver was accomplished. I reveled in its spinning, whirring sound, knowing someday I would accomplish this feat myself.

Talk about a pecking order, we had seating order. Mom and Dad always got the swing and we children had our repective places on the front steps. The dog was the one who didn't seem to care just where he went. He only wanted to be close to anyone who would scratch his ears while talking to him in a soft voice.

Front porches can be fun even when you are alone. It was a favorite place to build a fort from blankets thrown over chairs where you could conquer all sorts of imaginary enemies. You could even hide from your friends behind the ivy, while they fruitlessly searched for you in the front- and backyard. It can also be the setting for a large display of dolls for your sisters and all the paraphernalia that come with those sort of things. Being a guy, I never really knew all the details.

Today's modern builders have no idea how many relationships have failed to develop for lack of a porch swing. Moonlit summer nights when the moonbeams danced on the floor of the porch through the rustling ivy made even the shyest boy bolder, and his companions more receptive. Just ask your mom, dad, or grandparents.

I'm sure my reflections and ideas will do little to bring about the return of the old-style front porch. Modern-day builders are too interested in the bottom line. To them a porch is an added cost. The money saved can be spent elsewhere, so hours of pleasure—which money cannot buy—will be lost by the homeowner.

If you're planning to build a house, don't forget to leave room for a large, handsomely made porch swing. One that will squeak at just the right point in its swaying motion. You will never regret it and neither will your children.

BALLET OF FLIGHT

One of nature's most exquisite sights is a flock
of snowbirds flying in one of their perfectly
timed, tight, rhythmic formations.

The brilliant winter's sun reflecting
in flashes off their tiny forms
only adds to their aura.

Appearing almost joyful, they
twist, turn, and flair in perfect unison,
buoyed by the crisp cold air.

The whirring sound emitted from swiftly
beating wings punctuates their
flawless orchestrated ballet.

The heavenly choreographer hiding somewhere
in the early morning mist is as pleased as
you with their delicate performance.

You wait with anticipation for an encore,
for you know real prima ballerinas
always appear for a final bow.

James A. Nelson

STEPS OF LIFE

We all take life's first step. Mine was at age one.
Boy was it fun!

My second step came at six. The start of school.
What a trip!

My third step was college. To gain further knowledge.

My fourth step came at 22. Uncle Sam said,
"You must do your duty too."

My fifth step was at 25. I came home
and was married. It was great to be alive!

My sixth step came at 27. My first child was born.
I was in heaven!

My seventh step came three children later,
each child adding a best-selling chapter to my life's pages.

My eighth step was at 42. I came home one night
and my wife said, "I don't need you."

My ninth step was at 61. Who knows
perhaps there is another one.

My tenth step came when I realized
each step in life is for better or worse.

Aren't you glad you took the first?

James A. Nelson

CONGRESS OF THE UNITED STATES
HOUSE OF REPRESENTATIVES
WASHINGTON, D.C. 20515

GEORGE R. NETHERCUTT, JR.   April 13, 1998
WASHINGTON

Mr. James Nelson
6119 N. Colton Street #13
Spokane, Washington 99207

Dear James:

    Thank you for sending me a copy of an article
you wrote entitled "Adversity Builds Character and
Strong Families." I appreciate receiving this and
agree with you that adversity whatever the kind is a
catalyst for many good things. I hope you share
your concern and admonitions with others.

    Best regards.

                              Cordially,

                              GEORGE R. NETHERCUTT, JR.
                              Representative in Congress

GRN:scj

Thanks for your thoughts on this, Jim!

ADVERSITY BUILDS CHARACTER AND STRONG FAMILIES

Through the years I have often watched as humans rally around each other in times of adversity. This support has not only extended to individuals in different needy circumstances, but to the populace as a whole in events like natural catastrophes. A feeling of camaraderie and actual giving in all forms is extended by one and all.

While these past events have been emotionally satisfying, none can compare to the unity of the populace here and worldwide during the World War II years. Everyone became involved. It's not surprising that crime rates were low and divorce was almost nonexistent.

Hardly a family was untouched when it came to having a loved one put in harm's way during this period. Those still at home were actively engaged in projects to further victory for us and our allies—from women working in defense plants (Rosie the Riveter) to the female oilers in the bustling freight yards. Let's not forget the mothers at home who saved cooking grease that could be reused in the manufacturing of munitions. They also made do with ration coupons for sugar, butter, and other staples. Meat stamps were also a high priority. Children, such as I, were often members of victory-oriented organizations. These organizations consisted of young people who collected scrap metal, used rubber tires, tin foil and whatever else that could be used in the war effort.

Gangs did not have a place in this time period, since families were still functioning as well-knit units. The "me" attitude had not yet been spawned. A natural high was experienced not from a plant or chemical substance, but brought about by working to achieve victory and an eventual return home to our loved ones, not to mention freedom from oppression for the rest of the world.

Marriages lasted because the men who had been tempered on the battlefield learned how to accept responsibility in all matters. The women at home, who faced years of lonely separation from husbands and lovers, felt that their families and planned futures were worth every sacrifice they had to endure.

An average day started with the morning paper capsulating all the news from the different fronts. There was little space in the main news for much else. Besides, tragedies like the Oklahoma City and Trade Center bombings were unheard of. Personalities who create these types of holocausts had not yet developed in the United States.

The common bond of eventual victory consumed everyone in the free world. The President's sex life wouldn't have gained one inch of space in your local newspaper or one sentence on the national TV news during this time. No one had time for petty partisanship. The people believed in each other, not in gossip or innuendo.

Evenings were taken up with a family dinner—you know, the kind where everyone sits down together, eats, and has an actual fruitful conversation. An exodus to the living room followed dinner so we could listen to the radio and to radio news commentators such as Gabriel Heater, Edward R. Morrow's "This is London" and Walter Winchell's "Good Evening Mr. and Mrs. America and All the Ships at Sea" while Morse code dit-dotted in the background. They were our eyes and ears of the war. Our doors were never locked and policemen still walked neighborhood beats, twirling their nightsticks by those leather thongs. I never did understand how they mastered this maneuver. I still don't.

Baseball was played in the streets and ice-skating was allowed on natural ponds as well as on a multitude of man-made flooded areas. A litigious society that now hampers such activity had not materialized. If they got hurt someone accepted the responsibility of their own actions. They did not look for a victim to blame. Other things were more important, like "Is my father, brother, uncle, or cousin sleeping safe tonight—or even alive, for that matter?"

I remember walking into the kitchen one Saturday morning and my Mother was crying. "What's wrong, Mom?" I asked. Choking back tears she said, "Mrs. Donahue put up two gold stars today, Jimmy." "What are gold stars, Mom?" I asked. She then explained to me that families who had someone in the service displayed a red pennant with blue stars on a white field for each member in the service. So I asked, "What about the gold stars?" She started crying once more when she said, "The gold stars represent a member of the family who was killed in action." "You don't mean. . ." She didn't let me finish. "She lost two sons last week and that leaves only one." I started to cry also. The news brought tears to this neighborhood for blocks around. Yes, adversity does make for stronger families.

Prayer in school was as common as the flag salute. They were seldom missed at home either. After all, my two uncles, in faraway places, needed all the prayers they could get.

Thoughts like What can I do to help? were uppermost in people's minds. It was easy to recruit Air Raid Wardens, Coast Watchers, and volunteers to wrap bandages or to serve coffee and doughnuts at the U.S.O. After all, we were all in this together. My Father, an Air Raid Block Warden, was too old to be drafted. He and thousands like him took their positions quite seriously.

He often went out at night to participate in Air Raid drills. His white helmet and white armband were like friendly beacons in the darkness to the neighbors gathered behind curtained windows. All light had to be shielded from the outside. The Air Raid siren's mournful wailing could be heard all over town; especially Wednesday at noon, as they all blew in unison so civil defense personnel could be sure they were operational.

Singles bars would have had a difficult time making it during the war years. People met through mutual friends, U.S.O. dances, or if you were so inclined, church. The dances allowed you to hold someone close and sway with the music. Like they used to say, "Swing and Sway with Sammy Kaye." It's much more romantic than standing several feet apart as you dance. Besides, you didn't have to yell at each other so you could be heard over the amplified music. We thought Harry James' trumpet was loud enough when he broke into "Moonlight Serenade," "Begin the Beguine" or "Cherri-Berri-Bin." These were only a few.

Tommy Dorsey's muted trombone was like gentle rain from heaven. I never could convince my children that playing music loud didn't make it sound better. I'm sure I'm not alone in this thankless endeavor.

We now have new technology that has made life physically easier and inflation that has made it necessary for both men and women to work to attain the American dream. The feeling of unity everyone had during the war only comes spasmodically in this day and age, only when disasters strike, but I know this is only human nature. We shouldn't have to have earth-shattering events to bring about the benevolent behavior brought about by trying times. It should be instilled in us from the cradle to the grave, regardless of circumstances. These valuable human traits are in us all but must be nurtured by parental guidance and moral values learned as we develop. Families must again function as a unit and establish goals towards this end.

Social systems that create lack of values and other demeaning attributes must be revamped to allow attainable goals for us all. Not the goal of victory on the battlefield, but the goal of extending a helping hand to others and oneself. The rebirth of the American family is attainable.

As much as politicians would like to make you believe, they are not the source one should look to for the return of family values. It will only happen if parents, single parents, and extended families, being good role models themselves, work with their children towards these ideals, in the confines of a stable home.

SO, IT'S ONLY A TABLECLOTH

As I gingerly brushed the crumbs from my red and white checkered tablecloth in my bachelor apartment, my mind began to reflect. "There is much more to a checkered tablecloth than the pattern," I thought. Grandma's was red and white fifty years ago.

It covered her large dark oak table with a warm flair. She would tenderly place it with loving care before each meal. It was barely large enough to cover to the table's corners, even though she had made it herself to accommodate her large family—ten children, Grandpa, and herself.

She felt a proper tablecloth was as important as the meal, and all of us around her large oak table agreed. The pot roast set before us, surrounded with potatoes and carrots simmering in their own juices would not have looked right without a proper tablecloth. I'm sure the Thanksgiving turkey would have walked away if not presented on the proper table spread.

"So, it's only a tablecloth, you say. Don't let your Grandma hear you say that," Grandpa would answer, "or she'll box your ears." Of course, no one really felt threatened at this statement because Grandma wouldn't box anybody's ears, let alone a grandchild's. She could swing a mean lilac switch with accuracy across bare legs if a grandchild misbehaved, but box someone's ears—never.

I enjoyed so many meals at Grandma's house growing up. Seems like we ate every holiday meal in her large dining room. How does the song go? "Over the hills and through the woods to Grandmother's house we go."

The big old iron Monarch cookstove in the kitchen is what she cooked her masterpieces on. From your basic foods to apple pie with golden crusts that would melt in your mouth. Believe me, they weren't fat free. All this was done with nothing but a thermometer on the heavy oven door. I guess you could say it was cooking by the seat of your pants. I remember the wood crackling and seeing the coals falling as I peered through the draft on the side of the stove. It tickled me because it was my job to split the kindling and set the fire the night before when I stayed overnight. It was a chore I loved to do and couldn't do at home.

My mother had one of those newfangled electric stoves. To tell you a secret, she couldn't cook or bake as well as Grandma. Sure, the linoleum floor was cold to my bare feet in the early morning but the heat generated by the stove, combined with Grandma's love, would keep any barefooted grandchild warm.

It was always the grandkid's job to set the table for the family gatherings. I would eagerly volunteer to spread the tablecloth. No, I'm not talking red and white checks now. I weny to her fine-linen chest and pick out the finest-patterned white linen one I could find. I liked the one for Christmas with the holiday-bells and holly-wreaths design woven into the fine linen the best. The tablecloth itself just reeked with the Christmas spirit. Especially after it suffered a few gravy and cranberry stains.

On other occasions we had a choice of beautiful embroidered tablecloths, as well as colored ones that would hurt your eyes when the dining room light was just right. So Grandma kept the light on medium or low most of the time. When I asked why, she answered, "For atmosphere." I wasn't sure what atmosphere was at my young age but I knew whatever it was it seemed to make the food even more palatable and the conversation softer.

For everyday use the red and white one was her tablecloth of choice. She told me once, "It just seems to belong. Besides, it almost matches my apron." The red and white striped apron she was never without was as much a part of her as her massive grandma arms that would hug me before bedtime—after we said our prayers.

As I grew older and ventured out on my own I have never been without a red and white checkered tablecloth. When my future wife and I were dating we often ate at my small dining room table, which was never without an appropriate, handsome tablecloth. I hadn't yet built my dream home but my tablecloth was always perfectly acceptable. We shared many toasts through lighted candles as we developed our physical and emotional bonding. I also made sure the room was dimly lit. What did Grandma call it—"atmosphere?"

After we were married my wife ventured home with a blue and white checked one. I took one look at it and said, "Hon, you must return the tablecloth." She looked at me in hurt surprise. "So, it's only a tablecloth. What's the big fuss about the color?" Without hesitation I began to tell her the story about Grandma's tablecloths—something I had failed to do earlier. Before I was done she was folding up the blue and white tablecloth tenderly and saying, "I'll be right back, dear."

Two hours later she returned with a smile and a large package, from which she removed and gently laid before me a red and white tablecloth. Then once more she reached into the sack smiling. "What is she bringing out now?" I thought. Lo and behold—and where she found it I never will know—with utmost womanly tenderness she began to spread a white linen tablecloth on our recently acquired oak table, making sure it reached to all the corners evenly, just like Grandma would do. Smiling to myself I thought, "She would sure look good in a red and white striped apron."

I could only react with shocked surprise when I noticed the large Christmas bells, surrounded by boughs of holly, scattered through the glistening white linen. I choked up just a little, since men don't cry, and looked up at her saying, "Where in the world did you find it?" It was July and I knew no stores would be featuring a Christmas-spirit-filled item such as this fine tablecloth. Slowly she wrapped her arms around my waist and with a gentle squeeze looked up into my misty eyes and said simply, "Merry Christmas, Jim, from Grandma."

THE GENTLE WARMTH OF A FIRE CAN ALSO WARM YOUR SOUL

Have you ever noticed that bonfires and campfires create heat for the body as well as warmth for the soul?

Bonfires are for short, pleasurable outings. Campfires are normally larger and built for overnight stays. If you disagree with my terminology, feel free to use your own. Either of these outdoor fires generally means fun times for everyone involved. A bonfire near an outdoor skating pond at night was my favorite.

You could always see laughing people of all ages darting in and out of the dancing shadows created by the fire. Quite often they were clutching a cup of coffee or hot chocolate; this was done for warming their insides as well as their hands. The vision of steam rising from the skater's damp clothes as they gathered around the campfire, combined with the pungent smell of wool drying, completed the scene. The cold crisp nights that produced the best ice conditions, also made possible a breathtaking display from the heavens. Every star was a twinkler and you knew if you were just a little taller you could reach out and touch one.

Who can forget that moment when you noticed that cute girl across the ice? She was laughing while drinking hot chocolate and trying to balance on her skates at the same time. Her comical movements caused you to laugh also. You couldn't tell the color of her hair because it was tucked up under her wooly stocking cap. The bulky knit scarf that snuggled around her soft, girlish neck only made her look more mysterious. Her cheeks were flushed a rosy red from the cold air and she looked like "fun."

If things went well tonight, you thought, perhaps she would accept your offer for a skate and in your mind's eye the two of you, with clasped hands, would move in perfect harmony around the pond. Your long walk home that night would be so much easier if that cute girl was going in your direction. If you both could stop laughing long enough, you could stop to see who could blow their breath the farthest. Of course you would let her win. Perhaps when you reached her front porch, if you were lucky, she'd let you steal a kiss. Surely the campfire you were sitting by, when you first saw her through the flames, not only brought heat to your body but warmth to your soul.

I must not forget the ever present marshmallow. I know the only reason they were even put on the earth was to be the fun food at most bonfires and campfires. You seldom cooked a perfect marshmallow. The roasting stick you used was either too short, too long, too limp, too fat, or too slim to allow you the correct distance from the fire. Usually the marshmallow would turn black, bubbly, and mushy, but no one cared. Certainly not I! Most could hardly wait to get these tasty morsels into their mouths. This often led to burnt tongues and watery eyes. The beginner who failed to blow on them first suffered more than the experienced, cautious ones who knew procedure was necessary.

Bonfires at a wiener roast were also special. As you grew older this event often took on a romantic flair. At these teenage gatherings you still consumed hot dogs with lots of relish and catsup, but few onions. Marshmallows were also available and perhaps a smattering of spirits. The conversation among the girls would drift from who likes whom, to "Isn't he cute."

The boys were more inclined to talk sports, but were not immune to statements like, "Do you think she likes me?" and "I wonder if she would give me her phone number?" As the evening wore on, hands that once held only coffee cups, or hot chocolate with perhaps a smattering of spirits, now began to reach out into the darkness, searching for the warm grasp of another. Many lifetime commitments began around campfires such as these. If you don't believe me just ask your mom, dad, or grandmother.

There is nothing quite like a campfire in a hunting camp, blessed with the odor of frying bacon in the morning and a hunter's stew bubbling in a cast-iron pan at the edge of the fire in the evening. Don't forget the coffeepot, which also sits at the edge of the fire and always seems to have just one more cup in its cavernous belly, since it completes the scene. Because of the isolation it's easy to build a large fire. The kind where you can't stand close because of the intense heat, so you stand back and your backside gets cold. A smaller fire would be more practical but not nearly as friendly. A hunting campfire must be built with large, heavy logs. As these large logs burn and fall together a shower of sparks explodes skyward looking like thousands of fireflies in the darkness. All eyes follow these minute pieces of fire as they rise towards the heavens, each person lost in his own thoughts, remembering other hunts and other fires shared with the same group, gathered around in this moment in time. The young hunter nestled in his sleeping bag nearby is happily listening to all the stories being told by his elders. Perhaps tomorrow he will get a buck and have his own story to tell. The snapping sound of burning tamarack soon lulls him to sleep.

Let's not forget the bonfire built for the casual childhood sleep-over in the backyard. Dad is usually in charge of the fire and the cutting of the roasting sticks. This is always a chore because every one has to be just right—you know, custom cut for size and age of the prospective holder. Have you ever tried to show a child how to roast a marshmallow? Unfortunately it's not a skill you are born with. An occasional tear will appear as the marshmallows continue to drop off the stick and fall into the fire. But after a little comforting and advice there's always another try.

Dad and Mom are often forced to tell the older children to let the smaller ones closer to the fire. After all, they all must go through the learning process. Ghost stories are eagerly told and everyone glances around to see if fright has appeared in the expressions of their gathered friends.

As the fire dies down all retire to their sleeping bags. By this time the backyard will be littered with burnt roasting sticks. Most still have small bits of marshmallow stuck to their charred tips. This is okay because you know all the sticks represent sleeping children, cozy and warm in their sleeping bags, smiling as they sleep and dreaming of that perfectly roasted marshmallow.

Empty wiener bags are also scattered about the yard. Mom will smile when she comes out later and cleans up the area on her final bed check. Moms have a habit of doing this sort of thing. As she hesitates, smiles, and takes a last look at the ashes from the fire, perhaps she is remembering that high school wiener roast she and Dad attended long ago—when in one magical moment his hand reached out in the darkness and found hers.

Yes. Bonfires do warm your body as well as your soul.

A PLACE IN THE SUN

When I was very young my parents always told me,
Child, you must find your place in the sun.

When I reached the magical age of 21, I felt,
surely I had found my place in the sun.

At 41, after marriage and four wonderful children,
Perhaps I had found my place in the sun.

At 61, alone, except for my children and
seven beautiful grandchildren, I was peaceful
with the fact this must be my place in the sun.

At 71, gazing out my large living room
window I began to ponder. Did I really ever
find my place in the sun?

My answer came heaven sent,
as the afternoon sun began to creep across
the tufted carpet towards my rocking chair.

When the warmth from the sun's gentle rays
began to caress my stocking feet, I wept.
At last, I knew I had found my place in the sun.

James A. Nelson

LIFE'S REFLECTIONS

Your eyes are the windows

to your soul and the pathway

to your heart.

They mirror your joys

with their twinkle and

your sorrows with their tears.

No matter what their color,

they make life's beauty and

its struggles much easier to bear.

During life's journey, they often

determine your choice of mate

and where you plant your roots.

Yes, your eyes are the reflection

of your life.

James A. Nelson

INNOCENCE

Yes, a good girl is hard to find,
and it often takes a great deal of time.

Most girls have that shy look of innocence.
A look of untouched sweetness.
A good girl is hard to find.

A sparkling smile combined
with subtle grace, are always pluses.
A good girl is hard to find.

Put them all together
and your choice can only be,
a woman, who still warmly blushes.

Yes, a good woman is hard to find.

James A. Nelson

THE SCENT OF A WOMAN

Yes, there is the scent of a woman.

It's the scent of her lingering perfume

after she leaves a room.

It's the fresh scent of her warm, tender body

lying receptively in your bed,

after her nightly shower, before she sleeps.

It's the sweet scent of her soft hair as she

lies next to you through long nights.

It's the scent of togetherness,

your two bodies intertwined.

Knowing she will always be there.

Then she leaves, and all that's left

is the scent of a woman.

James A. Nelson

THE SOUND OF A WOMAN

Yes, there is a sound of a woman.
It's a soothing soft voice,
whispering words of endearment,
reaching your ears in the darkness
of a sleepless night.
Words easily described but
difficult to duplicate.

A voice that rings with tender mother's love
as she speaks the names of her children,
then changes to a voice that
trembles with a different passion,
when quiet times are shared.

Her bubbling laughter is more
melodious than the blue bird's song,
reminding you of spring.
its sweet melody sounding like
the overture to the concert of summer.

The sound of a woman is with you
from the beginning of your life
and throughout its span.
Ending with the voice of the woman
who meant so much,
continuing to echo,
with it' simple, quiet, good-bye.

James A. Nelson

THE INNOCENT EYES
OF CHRISTMAS

Red, blue and green Christmas
lights shine twice as bright,
through the innocent eyes of a child.

Santa, his reindeer and his home
at the North Pole are easily seen
through the innocent eyes of a child.

Christmas trees stand taller,
their crowning angels so much brighter,
through the innocent eyes of a child.

The piles of gifts askew, beneath the tree's
brightly adorned boughs, appear twice as large,
through the innocent eyes of a child.

Families gathered around the tree's fragrant
silhouette generate warmth, spirit, and togetherness,
through the innocent eyes of a child.

Christmas passes year after year and
too soon, you no longer see the season,
through the innocent eyes of a child.

Suddenly your body is old but your Christmas
spirit remains intact. You experience the joys and
now some sorrows of seasons past. Yet, only
on this Holy night, you still see Christmas
through the innocent eyes of a child.

James A. Nelson

"I'LL BE HOME FOR CHRISTMAS"

It was late at night on December 21, 1954, in a Boston bar, when I first heard the song, "I'll Be Home For Christmas." I couldn't help myself; I set my Knickerbocker beer down on the table and started to cry. My five buddies, all dressed in the khaki uniform of the U.S. Army, as I was, looked at me in surprise. After all, we were part of one of Uncle Sam's finest units, bloused combat boots and all and we certainly didn't cry in public. My friend Bill looked at me and said, "What the hell is wrong with you, Nelson? You're going home tomorrow, discharge in hand." "I know," I replied, "I guess it's just been so damn long since I've been there and there were times when I didn't think it would ever happen." They all grinned, hoisted their Knickerbockers in salute and said in a chorus, "Well it did, and we're here to see you put some wings to that song, 'I'll Be Home For Christmas.'" By this time, I was laughing and all was right with my world once again.

Early the next morning, I boarded a silver-colored DC-3 with Mohawk Airlines emblazoned on the sides and tail. It was the prettiest plane I had ever laid eyes on, I thought as we raced down the runway headed for New York. I had confirmed reservations to LaGuardia, but after that I was flying standby in the busiest time of the year. Just two days before Christmas. Maybe, just maybe, I would make it home for Christmas after all, I reflected. The flight was uneventful but bumpy, characteristic of the DC-3.

After landing, I bought a black stuffed poodle for Lois, my fiancée, then headed for the ticket counter of an airline I was familiar with. The maze and confusion of the Christmas rush were all around me. I crossed my fingers and said to the ticket agent, "I need a ticket to Spokane, Washington. The smiling ticket agent said, "Going home for Christmas, soldier?" I looked at him and said, "I'm not sure, as I'm flying standby and I've got three thousand miles to go." While he stamped my ticket he said, "Throw your duffel bag on the conveyor belt and step over here. I want to tell you something." I replied, "Are you sure I'm going to get on that plane? I don't want to be separated from my duffel bag." "Damn it," he said, "put it on the belt. You're going to be on that plane." I grinned as I threw that big old bag on the belt. It weighed almost as much as I did. He then pulled me aside and said, "When you get on the plane tell the stewardess—that's what they were called in the '50's—you're going home for Christmas and you definitely need a seat." I thanked him and waved as I started down the concourse towards a Boeing StratoCruiser sitting on the tarmac.

After climbing the stairs to the plane's door I was met by a stewardess. She looked pretty and cute in her neat little uniform— they always do. With a smile on her face she asked, "Going home, soldier?" I grinned and said, "I hope so," as I relayed the ticket agent's instructions to her. She grabbed my hand and said, "Come with me." She then proceeded to take me down a small staircase, which led to the cocktail lounge in the plane's belly. While we were standing on the staircase she said, "You sit here till we're in the air and leveled off, then go into the lounge and grab a stool. That will be your seat for the rest of the flight." Seemed a bit unorthodox but certainly reasonable to a soldier who hadn't been home for a long time.

The lounge was enjoyable but as we neared Chicago I thought, "I sure hope I get a regular seat for the rest of my flight." Then I remembered I was changing planes in Chicago. "I will get a seat," I thought confidently.

During my long and pleasant flight in the lounge I met a very attractive woman in a fur coat. She also had on one of those cute little matching hats. We talked for several hours as we sat in the lounge. She told me she was getting off in Chicago. All at once the intercom announced our arrival at O'Hare. As she got up to leave she knelt down, leaned toward me and whispered, "How would you like to spend Christmas with me, Jim?" I was caught by surprise and didn't quite know what to say. Finally I said, "Thanks, but I have a fiancée and family waiting for me at home a couple of thousand miles down the road. I really must go on." She reached out, gave my arm a gentle squeeze and said, "Have a good life, soldier." She then walked up the stairs, off the plane into the darkness of the black winter night. We were like two ships in the night. Their blinking lights saying, "What a wonderful interlude in two people's lives."

I left the plane and boarded a Lockheed Electra for the final leg of my journey home. This plane soon lulled me to sleep with the hum of its perfectly pitched props. When I awoke we were in darkness, flying low over the state of Montana. Lights shining from the scattered ranch windows glowed like a bright warm blanket as it spread over the sparkling snow. This seasonal scene only enhanced my desire to be home for Christmas with loved ones.

I arrived home at 8:30 A.M. after a total of twenty-four hours, from Worchester, Massachusetts, counting the layovers and plane changes. I grabbed a bite to eat at the airport and then hailed a cab into town. No one knew I was coming, therefore no one met me. I wanted to surprise all of them.

My fiancée, Lois, worked as an elevator operator in a large department store and that's where I headed, as fast as possible. Leaving my gear in the cab I told the driver, "Wait for me, I won't be long," and entered the store.

As I approached the elevators I noticed a supervisor standing in front of the elevators. I walked up to her and asked, "Could you tell me which elevator Lois is operating?" She looked at my uniform and said, "You must be Jim, I have heard all about you for a long time." Smiling, I replied, "Yes, I'm Jim and Lois doesn't know I'm home." She replied, "She's on elevator six." As I walked towards the elevator she called after me, "Give her a hug for me."

As I stood in front of the elevator I wondered, "What will I say to her when she opens the door?" I hadn't rehearsed a thing. The door finally opened and the passengers scurried off into the Christmas rush. This left Lois standing there alone and looking at me with shocked surprise. If anything, she was prettier than I remembered, her face framed by her flaxen-colored hair. It flowed down over her shoulders and cascaded almost to her waist. I had always had a penchant for blondes. As her face turned a warm red, she started to cry and as the tears rolled down her cheeks she said, "What are you doing here? You never told me you were coming home." I knew then what I was going to say. I took her in my arms and with tears in my eyes also, said, "Honey, haven't you heard that Christmas song, 'I'll Be Home For Christmas?' Well, here I am."

With that, the supervisor closed the elevator doors with a clatter, leaving us in semi-darkness and alone. All at once, off in the distance, I swear I heard a laughing voice saying, "Merry Christmas to All and to All a Good Night."

A FAMILY TREASURE

*She is small, pink, dainty, and very special
from her tiny fingers down to her perfect toes.
For she is your firstborn.*

*You know as you gaze at her with wonder,
she will be loved, cuddled, pampered, and cajoled.*

*The other love in your life looks at her with
the soft, tender, bonding eyes of motherhood.*

*Your marriage is now complete,
fulfilled and consummated.
For she is your firstborn.*

*Life will hold many highs and lows
For this bundle of soft skin.
Complete with clinging arms and grasping fingers.
Oh, so warm with their total dependency.*

*This perfect miniature family treasure,
will grow tall and strong and make you proud.*

*They say nothing in life remains the same,
but this is not always true.
For she will always be your firstborn.*

James A. Nelson

A FAMILY TREASURE

As my wife and I started out the door of our small apartment I heard the inevitable. "Jim, have you got the diaper bag, the food bag, the clothes bag, the car seat, and above all don't forget the extra pacifier?" Without a doubt we now had become a family. We were about to venture out, with our six-week-old daughter, on our first outing into the world of parenthood.

Smiling, though bent double from all the paraphernalia, I watched my wife walking with confident strides toward our car. All she carried was a soft bundle of responsibility, something she carried so well during motherhood. She grasped responsibility almost as tight as the five tiny, strong fingers that grasped her single finger inside the pink blanket. It was the finger she had placed inside the baby's blanket for "baby reassurance."

We are now reaping the benefits of marriage and our biological urges. I say benefit, because the sleepless nights and responsibilities will be with you until your newborn becomes an adult. The benefits come during a lifetime of love and sharing with your own family throughout your lifetime.

There are all kinds of experts in the field of parenthood but nothing can compare to common-sense, actual hands-on experience, and a worn copy of Dr. Spock. Ours was given to us by in-laws, inscribed with these words, "We raised the new Mother with this book of wisdom and the world is happy with the finished product." "They couldn't have been more correct," I thought to myself.

In actuality nothing can really prepare you for the joys and trials of parenthood. I'm sure it's an inborn trait that has lain sleeping during your young life but is awakened with a soft but loud cry when you happen to be blessed with a child. Even a childless couple has these traits which are stirred, awakened, and developed with each contact they have with other's children. After all, they are no different than parents except that, either by design or chance, they haven't shared the experience of raising a child.

It is difficult to write an essay on raising a child. Most of all because so many experiences you felt were a crisis at the time became merely laughing matters as the years progress. You have heard the expression, "You will laugh at this years from now," or words to that effect. I certainly didn't think it was a laughing matter when our bundle of joy rolled off the bed and hit the floor with a startled cry and loss of breath. I learned you can't take your eyes off them for a second— and certainly not a minute!

You will ask yourself a million times Should I have done that? or Should I do this? Guilt will creep into your life over so many trivial matters. Like the time you forgot to double-check the pins in a diaper. Then you are met with a cry of pain from a tiny voice. "How could you have possibly done that?" you ask yourself.

Today the pin problem has almost disappeared with the advent of disposable diapers. Only one of the material things that have made raising a child so much easier in this age of technology. No more pans of hot water to heat a bottle or baby's first solid food. In this matter the microwave has become a blessing to all, including the baby who is making it known through vocal expression that it's "time to eat — now!"

You can read all the books and listen to all the advice, professional and nonprofessional but nothing will replace the lessons learned and confidence gained through actual child-raising experience. It will prepare you for most any trial in life. It will make you smile and mold your character with strength you never knew you possessed. After all, there is nothing more concerning than facing the unknown.

I feel because I have been a parent four times I fit the mold and the products we produced and formed have made us proud.
I would like to end this piece with a poem but actually it is more than that. It is an expression of love and attachment most often so difficult to explain in words but I will try.

She is small, pink, dainty, and very special
from her tiny fingers down to her perfect toes.
For she is your firstborn.

You know as you gaze at her with wonder,
she will be loved, cuddled, pampered, and cajoled.
For she is your firstborn.

The other love in your life looks at her with
the soft, tender, bonding eyes of motherhood.
For she is your firstborn.

Your marriage is now complete,
fulfilled and consummated.
For she is your firstborn.

Life will hold many twists, turns, highs
and lows for this bundle of soft skin complete
with green eyes and curly, silky blond hair.
For she is your firstborn.

This perfect miniature family treasure,
will grow tall and strong and make you proud.
For she is your First Born.

They say nothing in life remains the same,
but this is not always true.
For she will always be your firstborn.

I hope all you parents will accept this poem in its generic sense, since all of you have your very own firstborn. During your own parenting experience you will have your trials and triumphs, none of which will seem trivial at the time. But in the long run you will never regret it—good luck—you'll need it.

A SMALL WILD TREASURE

"Hi Lois, kids, come see what Dad has brought home," I yelled, as I came through the back door. Carrying a cardboard box with a small, precious, soft animal sleeping inside. I was almost afraid to put it down.

Lois, my wife, was the first one into the kitchen as I gently set the box on the floor. She took one look and said, "Oh Jim, it's a baby deer and it's so little." "About two pounds," I said. "I got it about an hour ago from the state game warden. He called me at work and asked if I would give it a home for about five months. Someone had brought it into their office and they had no place to keep it. In September they will pick it up and place it in a game refuge. A safe home for animals after they are old enough to take care of themselves," I explained. One by one my three children, Kim (10), Lori (8), and Merri (5)5, rushed into the kitchen. I had never heard so many gleeful sounds and so many questions as they gazed down at the tiny animal. "Where did you get it?" "Can I hold it?" "Not now," I said, "We have to wait until it gets used to us and her new home." By this time I had determined she was a girl deer, or *fawn* as baby deer are called. The questions kept coming. "Where did you find her?" "Can I hold her?" "Do we get to keep her?" "Where is she going to sleep?" "Whoa, hold on, one question at a time," I interrupted.

"I got her from the game warden because they had no place to keep her. For food we will feed her just like you would a baby or any small animal. Milk from a bottle to start and other food as she grows older. As for a name—I'll leave that up to you. I must get back to work." As I left I could still hear squeals of delight. The question, "What shall we name her?" followed me out the door to my car.

When I arrived home that evening Merri—so named because she had been born on Christmas—met me at the door. "Dad, I got to name her." I smiled and said, "Ok hon, what's her name?" "Faline," she said as she bounced up and down with excitement! "For sure," I said, "That's a great name. We all know about Bambi's mother, Faline. Let's hope that our Faline will grow up and have a baby of her own someday."

Now began five months of care and love enjoyed by the entire family. Faline was a constant joy. She was very clean, well mannered and quite loving. She took to us all but her favorite family member was Merri. That because Merri, who was home during the day, got to feed her most often, a job she loved to do. When she got hungry Faline would search her out with a bleating sound like a sheep. "Ba-ba-ba-ba." Only softer. After locating Merri she would remind her it was time to eat by gently nudging her with her head. Merri never tired of this job. Faline, staring at her with those soft brown eyes and making quiet loving sounds, rewarded her while she drank. Duke, our springer spaniel, became her instant protector and played this part throughout her stay in our big backyard. Anytime Faline became frightened she ran to his side. He gently licked her and gave her a mother's tender look and all would be right in her small world once more. To watch them play tag and wade together in the wading pool was always heartwarming.

Mittens, our cat, seldom noticed Faline and didn't like it when she danced and pranced in front of her, trying to make her run. After all, playing tag is fun even when you are a deer.

Her greatest treat was to go out in the backyard early in the morning and nip each new flower bud that had emerged in my wife's flower garden. Because we loved her we never scolded her. We knew these tasty flowers were part of her daily meals. In the wild she would be eating similar treats, including sweet-smelling clover buds and no one would correct her there. We laughed and said, "Faline is going outside for her dessert," as she headed for the door after she had her bottle. We wondered which buds or flowers she would choose first—roses, daises, or pansies? I always said pansies because these dainty little flowers were truly her favorite. You could almost see a smile on her face as she munched the colorful little flowers. Especially the yellow ones. Lois would be standing nearby with her hands on her hips, smiling, as Faline quietly ate up her flowers. Funny thing, in summers past if any one of us or our pets had damaged one of her plants we would not have been looked at with a smile. Faline just had a way of making everyone smile. We loved her and she often showed her love for us with a gentle nuzzle with her nose and a soft bleat, all the while staring at us with her dark eyes with those long lashes.

Her bedroom was Merri's room, where she slept on a blanket at the foot of her bed. Somehow she knew Merri, being the youngest in the family, needed her nighttime nearness. "She's like Merri's night light," I would say. "Too bad she doesn't have a shiny red nose like Rudolph the Red-Nosed Reindeer," we chuckled.

Our summer routine was made more fun as we watched her growing and playing in our big backyard. One afternoon I took her to the house of a friend who was raising a boy fawn for the game department also. Faline would have nothing to do with the little fawn and ran back to our station wagon. After all, she thought she was human like us.

The station wagon was one of her favorite places. She often took rides with us, all the while standing and looking out the windows in the back storage area. It was interesting and fun watching the other drivers as they passed us and viewed our back seat passenger. The looks we got were always happy ones, filled with surprise. Faline was a treasure and will always be remembered as part of our family.

Our parting came in late September. The game warden came to get her as he'd said he would. Lois, eight months pregnant at the time, was the only one home and she cried as the led Faline bleating out the door. My friend the warden called later to see if Lois was ok. Kim, Lori, and Merri shed a few tears when they returned home that evening. I knew I would miss her too. We knew this moment was coming and she was going to a good home. We were a better family because of Faline for all she did was give us her love, taking little in return.

About a year and a half later we received a nice letter and pictures from the refuge keeper where Faline was now living. The letter said, "Faline is our favorite deer. She always meets us when we drive into the refuge with apple treats. Her gentle bleat and moist nudge with her nose as she takes the apples gently from our hands makes our day. She is a real treasure. From the enclosed picture you will see she is now the proud mother of a little boy fawn we named Bambi." When Merri saw the pictures she jumped up and down and said, "Faline did grow up and have a baby named Bambi just as we knew she would." "Just like in the story," I said.

"Faline will be a good mother, won't she Dad?" Merri asked. "Without a doubt," I said. "You see, she is still doing the thing she knows how to do best, giving her love, only this time to Bambi and the refuge keepers."

LIFE IN THE FAST LANE

She was short, overweight, poorly dressed, and had a look of sadness about her. He was tall, thin, and attired in a dark pinstripe suit with a narrow red and blue striped tie held neatly in place with a gold tie tac. He had a briefcase in one hand and a Wall Street Journal tucked under his arm. He made an impressive sight with his graying hair. The teenager in the group had a ball cap pulled down over his eyes so you couldn't tell whether he was asleep or awake. I couldn't make out what was printed on his T-shirt—probably just as well. Only the cigarette dangling from his hand told me he was partially awake, as it hadn't slipped from his fingers.

All four of us were waiting at the bus stop for the 7:15 a.m. STA Express to downtown. We were all on different missions with different objectives but we had two things in common, *bus fare* and *life itself.*

As I often do with strangers I tried to determine something about the character of these casual transient fellow travelers, as we waited in overcast weather.

Right on time we boarded the express one by one when it came to a slow rolling stop in front of our bench. Its doors swung open with their usual noisy pneumatic swishing sound. The smiling driver greeted us with "Good morning." The dumpy woman grunted something softly as she boarded that I failed to hear. Mr. Wall Street Journal smiled and answered, "It certainly is and today will be the first day of the rest of your life." I thought that rather strange. I would have expected something like, "Get into the market while you can, son."

The teenager, fully awake by this time, to my surprise courteously replied to his greeting with, "It sure is a dazzling day and I intend to make the most of it." With these words he turned and flipped his cigarette out through the bus's swiftly closing doors, barely missing me as it passed over my shoulder.

I uttered a hasty, unintelligible reply to the driver's salutation as the bus bolted forward, leaving me grabbing a seat to steady myself. I then started my precarious journey down the aisle towards a seat in the back of the bus, dodging outstretched legs in the aisle along with shopping bags, knapsacks, and other obstacles along the way. The swaying motion of the bus caused me to stagger in the narrow aisle before I reached a seat. Reminded me of a sailor heading for an open hatchway in heavy seas.

After I was seated I realized my other bus stop passengers had blended into the early-morning group already seated. It was pleasant to listen to the quiet undertone of human chatter as the bus made its journey toward the city center. It seemed many of the passengers were regulars and shared a certain camaraderie not often found on other modes of transportation.

One thing we all seemed to have in common was none of us would have any problems finding a parking place or paying a parking fee upon our arrival at our destination. Best of all, if we were late for work we could always say, "The bus was late." An excuse I hadn't used since high school.

Two ladies in front of me were busily discussing the previous night's TV entertainment. Seems like they both enjoyed Frazier but felt the news was "just too depressing."

While one busily knitted some booties for a newly expected grandchild, her younger friend spoke of how she could hardly wait to have grandchildren. All of this was garnered from their friendly conversation while I gazed at the heavy traffic out my window wondering if it would rain.

Being a grandfather, I could appreciate their feelings but didn't feel like butting into their conversation. They would be sharing this maternal grandparent feeling soon enough. After all, a grandchild is a loving, warm extension of your own life. Who wouldn't want to experience this joy in their lifetime? I surely did.

By this time I knew that the balding man across the aisle from me was named John and his seat partner, with the worn, shiny lunch pail in his lap, was Bill. They both liked the Seattle Mariners, for what ungodly reason I couldn't fathom. Maybe it was because maybe someday the Mariners might, just might, win a pennant. Smiling, I thought to myself, "That will be the day." But I guess it could happen.

John was expecting a raise at work and Bill wasn't real sure what he was going to have for dinner, except it would probably come out of a can or carton. "Oh, and did you know that the bus company was going to rearrange its routes again?" Bill asked. This, of course, brought a sigh of passenger resignation from John, along with these words, "What can you do? You can't fight city hall." Bill replied, "You can say that again and the STA is even tougher."

Our driver slowed dramatically when he noticed a woman, arms flailing, pushing a stroller towards our next stop. He smiled, leaned back and said so all of us could hear, "We can't leave that family behind." We all nodded accordingly.

Waiting patiently, we all watched the young woman trying to negotiate the bus's narrow entryway, banging the stroller on each step while trying so hard not to wake her sleeping child. Then a kindly man stepped forward and offered his assistance. Her face broke into a broad smile and she looked up at him and said softly, "Thank you." Another passenger moved over to make room for her and the stroller with its still sleeping passenger. As we pulled away from the curb and picked up speed I had a very warm feeling for my fellow travelers. I almost stood up and clapped but I didn't want to wake the baby. Two more lives accepted into the "fast lane" of life, unbeknownst to the sleeping child

The bus gently rocked and rolled towards its downtown destination, causing me to doze with its soothing motion. The muted sound of the occasional bell indicating that someone wanting to get off, only added to the relaxing atmosphere. Yes, I thought, as the poet Robert Frost said, "But I have miles to go and promises to keep before I sleep." I was brought out of my dream world with a start as the bus careened sharply around the corner into the terminal. Raindrops began to fall from the leaden sky as I prepared to leave the bus. I was glad I had brought my new, push-button, pop-up umbrella. I won't leave it on the bus today, I thought reassuringly.

Everyone was in a hurry to depart at this final destination. I glanced up and noticed Mr. Wall Street Journal, smiling with briefcase in hand, was first off the bus, but not before he said briefly to the driver, "Don't forget the market is going up, son." This is what I had expected him to say earlier. The driver smiled in a knowing way and told him to have a nice day. Silently the poorly dressed, dumpy woman passed the driver without a word or smile, still looking very sad.

The woman with the baby stroller again safely negotiated her tricky departure with help from the kind passenger. Best of all, the baby was still asleep.

Someone had awakened the sleeping teenager just in time for departure. He already had an unlighted cigarette in his mouth as he passed the driver and didn't speak. Walking by, I thanked the driver for the smooth pleasant trip and remembered to smile as I said, "I'll be here at 5:15." He replied with a smile, "I'll be here but only until the market gets high enough so I can retire."

Leaving the bus I popped my push-button umbrella with a snappy flair and headed through a light rain toward my destination. Smiling to myself I thought, "Into each life a little rain must fall." As I walked and listened to the tat-tat-tat of rain on my umbrella I wondered, why would anyone want to leave a fun job like driving a bus? Then I realized – like life itself the ride may not always be smooth on the 7:15 A.M. STA Express but I'm sure glad I caught the bus.

PEN & PAPER

My Dear Mandy,

Not long ago you made a statement to me in your usual ten-year-old childlike innocence. You had no idea your casual reply to a question I asked would have such a profound and thoughtful effect on me.

We had just finished dinner and I was reading a letter to you from your grandmother who now lives hundreds of miles away. It was a beautifully handwritten letter, one that I knew had been written with love and care. This was easily determined just by looking at its flowing scroll. As the letter ended she stated, "It would be nice if one of you older children would write grandma and grandpa a letter. We miss you all a lot since you have moved to the United States from Canada."

When I looked up from the letter I said to you, "Mandy, you should write your grandparents a letter." The response I got was quite surprising and a little upsetting when you said, "Oh, I'm not going to write them, Grandpa, I'm going to e-mail them very soon."

I immediately thought, Please God, don't let our computer-oriented society take away, from one so young, the pleasure of writing and receiving a handwritten letter from a friend or loved one.

Mandy, you must realize a letter is not really a letter unless it comes in an envelope. An envelope always holds the element of surprise. You know at once who it's from by the familiar handwriting on its face but the message inside remains your secret.

Your letter didn't come over a machine that everyone in the family has access to, especially your snoopy brothers and sisters. You know as you rush to your quiet place, envelope in hand, that its message will be yours and yours alone. The cold, dark, even print of an e-mail letter will never allow you the luxury of this warm feeling.

An e-mail letter does not allow a doting grandparent one of life's great pleasures. The vision of a grandchild struggling with small hands and a dull pencil, working to put thoughts on paper. Occasionally their tongues may even peek out between half-clenched teeth as they tackle this grown-up task. Somehow a child sitting at a computer, all prim and proper, does not paint the same heartwarming scene.

So Mandy, please don't e-mail your grandmother a letter. Write her one instead. Let your fingers grow tired and cramped with your efforts. She then will know it's a special gift from you, one that she and grandpa can share. For after she reads it she will place it next to his morning coffee. He will smile when he notices your new form of grown-up handwriting. The loops and curls in your pen strokes, showing just a hint of your blossoming femininity. He will view your new writing skills with mixed emotions, proud of your letter's new mature look but a wee bit sad, realizing his little granddaughter is growing up much too fast. I feel the same way.

I remember so well the letters I received from your grandmother when I was in the army. They were the one bright spot in my life during this trying time. I often chuckled over her misspelled words. It would have been disappointing if she had had a spell check. For each one of her mistakes was so much like her. It made me feel that

I must have been put on this earth just to protect and shelter this fragile woman whom I loved.

It was easy to imagine her face turning a warm red, as she struggled over each mistake, knowing it was wrong and feeling more and more inadequate because of it. I had assured her over the months that I had been gone that these mistakes only made me care for her more. I explained to her, I didn't love her for her spelling but for so many other reasons. It took some time but she finally believed me. I could tell because her letters became more like the woman I had grown to love even more during our long separation.

I would never have tucked an e-mail letter in my helmet, for it wouldn't have come with an envelope scented with her favorite perfume—a pleasant odor that reminded all of us of the girl back home. The envelope was always sealed with the faint imprint of her lipsticked lips and initialed S.W.A.K., meaning it had been sealed with a kiss. The sight of this envelope in my sergeant's hand at mail call always made my heart beat a little faster.

Her letter would be taken from my helmet many times and read, before it was discarded. This never happened until her next letter was received. Besides, the places where we were receiving mail were not what you would call computer-friendly, if you know what I mean.

So Mandy, please do not forsake the art of handwritten letters. Besides grandparents, someone else may be disappointed. For someday you may have a loved one far away who will be waiting patiently for a letter to tuck into his helmet. A letter that is sealed with a lipsticked kiss and scented with your favorite perfume, misspelled words and all.

Love you,
Grandpa Jim

MOLECULAR DATING

Grandparents often end up dating once again after many years of marriage due to the loss of their mate—as in my case, Grandma.

It was and still is a challenge to once again play the dating game as a grandparent. I have taken an episode from my current single lifestyle and tried to point out some of the pitfalls.

Casually I mentioned to my female friend, "I have to go home and cook dinner." She looked at me and said, "It won't take you long to nuke it." What do you mean, 'nuke it'? I replied. Surprised, she almost shouted, "Microwave it—microwave it!" She left off the word *stupid* but I know she was thinking it. "You have one, don't you?" she countered with disbelief in her voice.

I hung my head, embarrassed, and with a chagrinned quiver in my voice I admitted, "I don't own one." I felt like I had just confessed to a mortal sin. Relieved and free at last, I sighed. I could tell my character points had just plummeted in her eyes—*damn*.

Hard to believe that lack of a microwave would be tantamount to missing your daily shower on a hot summer day. I vowed then and there to buy one at my first opportunity.

Trying to regain at least some semblance of her lost favor, I smiled and explained, "I don't cook much but I do a lot of canning." "Oh really," she said with surprise, "so do I. What is your specialty?" Without hesitation and with a straight face I replied, "I open up a can of stew, a can of spaghetti, a can of beans, a can of soup, et cetera." She laughed and slapped my shoulder. Just maybe I had gained back some of her favor points. Nevertheless, I'm going to buy a microwave.

It wasn't that easy. My first step into molecular cooking was an adventure and a nightmare of sorts. It was almost as mind boggling as when I bought my first TV in the '50s. And all I had to master then was the on and off switch. But that is another story.

I had just read an article about microwave cooking in *USA Today* and it seemed so simple. I realized later that I should have bought the weekend edition, since it would have been more detailed, perhaps pointing out some of the pitfalls as well as the benefits. After all, who wants their steak coming out a sissy white all the time?

I learned early that the "well-done brown" look on a savory steak is lost forever in the bowels of a microwave oven. I learned this and other microwave facts through trial and error after I bought one. It wasn't easy to give up my old cooking habits.

The easy part was filling out the credit application and receiving my choice of a free case of coke or a gift certificate for fine dining at McDonald's. This included an entire family of four. If you had more than two kids either you or the wife didn't eat. But that is another matter—at least you could save the tip.

After watching endless cooking demonstrations I settled on a specific microwave oven that was supposed to do everything, at least that's what the salesman told me. I walked out of the store with male pride in my step realizing I no longer was a second rate citizen in the eyes of the community as well as my friend—I owned a microwave.

Since I had been single for many years my three daughters had often expressed a desire for me to own a microwave. One even went so far as to offer to buy one years ago and I said no. As I folded the bill for my microwave and put it in my wallet I thought, "That sure was a mistake."

I had gotten by all these years without a cookbook. Who needs a cookbook telling you how to add ingredients that the average male has never heard of? Add those difficult temperature settings and it only becomes more confusing.

Who needs all those fancy worded instructions when the only directions you need are, "Remove dinner from carton, cut a large slit across the main entrée and peel back the cover from the potatoes. Add butter and place in preheated 400-degree oven. Cook for 4 –7 minutes, occasionally stirring the vegetables."

No one has to go to cooking school or take home economics to follow these easy steps. Besides, when I went to high school a boy in home economics would have had to fight his way home every night after school. On weekends he would be forced to stay home and rest up for Monday's challenges.

After spending weeks practicing with my microwave, I decided to invite my female friend over for dinner. I would show her just how proficient I had become with this nuclear monster, this metal box that took up half the counter space in my kitchen.

I had chosen the most beautiful packaged dinners I could find in the frozen food department of a local supermarket. I have to admit the picture on the front of each package looked good enough to eat! With practice sometimes my dinners even came out close to looking like the pictures. She would be proud of me I thought, and smiled with pleasure.

I spent all day Saturday vacuuming, dusting and cleaning my small apartment. The lamp next to my coach flickered with pure pleasure when I hit it with the dust cloth. It has been so long, it seemed to sigh. If only my dinner goes well, I reflected, as I gazed around my squeaky-clean living quarters. I had never felt so domestic in my entire single life. I had run the entire gauntlet of emotions in anticipation of the coming evening's mysterious interlude and it was only three in the afternoon.

She arrived about seven thirty, carrying a bottle of red vintage wine and two candles. She set the wine on the table, turned to me and softly said, "Jim, may I please have your candleholders?" Caught by surprise, I reached under the sink and pulled out two empty Bud longnecks and began to wash them out. She smiled, shrugged her shoulders and snickered with what seemed like resigned acceptance. Hopefully I had pulled it off, I thought to myself, as I placed my Bud bottles on the table with a cavalier motion. At least I had remembered to buy a red and white-checkered oiled tablecloth at the five and dime store. This would add a classy flair.

After some small table talk and a few glasses of red wine I asked her if she was ready for dinner. She replied, "You bet! I haven't eaten all day and I am famished!" I took her arm and with masculine pride led her to the kitchen, which was only two steps away in my tiny apartment.

I graciously pulled out the metal folding chair and offered her a seat. Because I had wanted everything to be served piping hot I hadn't started to microwave our dinner yet. I should have suspected something was amiss when she made a slight choking sound after I asked her if she wanted Swanson, Healthy Choice or Stouffer's. She also looked surprised when I offered her a choice of chicken cordon bleu, roast beef, cajun chicken or swedish meatballs.

Ruefully she exclaimed, "Oh, you finally bought a microwave— and to think I looked forward to a home-cooked meal all day." Caught by surprise I could only think of one thing to say. "Do you want the regular serving or the Hungry Man portion?" This didn't bring a smile to her face.

After a quick dinner she excused herself and said, "I have to run. I have an early day tomorrow." I helped her on with her coat and she swept out the door, her coat billowing in the wind from her speedy departure. I shouted at her rapidly departing form and windblown hair, "Next time I'll have cherries jubilee for dessert." She never looked back.

The next time a woman asks me if I own a microwave—I won't answer. Unless she is my granddaughter.

THE END OF AN ERA

Kris Dony, of Mead, Washington had been promising herself for years to take a picture of the picturesque, dilapidated old barn built near her home during the Victorian era. She passed it daily to and from work and had grown quite fond of its charming character. Oh, the stories it could probably tell, she thought, for it must have been close to 100 years old. On the morning of October 16, 1991, as she rushed out the door for work, she impulsively grabbed her camera, saying to herself, "I'll get a picture of the old barn today even if I'm late for work." She stopped down the road, not far from her house and yes indeed, finally got her picture—mission accomplished. She knew her boss would forgive her for being late.

Around ten in the morning, she began hearing some disturbing breaking news reports on her radio at work. Strong winds were pushing some small brush fires out of control around Spokane, Washington into the surrounding timbered suburban areas. This meant her home and acreage could possibly be in danger, for she lived only a few miles away from some of the spreading fires that had begun to circle the city.

Growing concerned a few hours later as the bulletins persisted, she asked her supervisor for permission to go home. Permission was granted. Hopefully nothing would happen to disturb her family's peaceful country lifestyle, she hoped as she hurried toward her car. Driving home fast, she noticed the smoke billowing in what only a few hours ago had been a clear sky. Soon she passed the site of the old barn she had photographed only hours before. It had been flattened and scattered in all directions from the 65 mile-per-hour gale force winds sweeping across the wheat fields. Now she was frightened. She had no idea what was happening but she knew it was ominous.

She had no way of knowing Firestorm 1991 was rapidly taking shape, ending a long six days later on October 22, 1991.

It took a devastating toll on property and human life. Before it was extinguished 40,000 to 45,000 acres would be laid waste in eastern Washington and northern Idaho as well as 200,000 acres in western Montana, burning in all three states at once, almost a repeat of the great fire of 1910. It also claimed the lives of a pregnant woman and her unborn child fleeing from the inferno, along with that of a firefighter in northern Idaho.

In its wake the fire would consume 136 homes, along with hundreds of vehicles and outbuildings. The loss of livestock and wildlife was immeasurable. At its height, the fire's perimeter would stretch over 125 miles. Property damage valued in billions would be lost before this inferno was controlled and $245 million would be paid in government relief funds. This holocaust left the land charred black and covered with ashes. To most, it resembled the aftermath of a volcano eruption. Fortunately, Kris and her family suffered no losses; for this she counts her blessings.

Today her picture of the old barn hangs in a place of honor in her home. She often wonders as she gazes at the barn's weathered form, why she grabbed her camera the particular morning that she took the picture. She had passed its decaying shape so many times over the years and it had always been there. Why was she so driven on that particular day?

She doesn't have an answer to this perplexing question but she does love her picture; maybe the old barn and the era it represented just wanted to be remembered.

A JOURNEY HOME

Recently I witnessed a struggle by a small individual against what I felt were impossible odds.

This individual started his journey home, through what must have been the densest jungle ever encountered by anything or anyone. Slender green treelike spires seemed to reach the sky, and the surrounding dense undergrowth created a heavy, humid atmosphere. The day was at least 90 degrees and no breeze. After about three hours of up-and-down climbing, this individual finally fell from one of the tallest tree-like spires onto a flat, hard surface. If anything, this surface was even greener than the rest of the jungle. He became confused from the fall and began going in circles. After his head cleared, he began feeling quite safe. Once again he started across the hard green surface at a fast pace, happy in the knowledge he would be home soon.

But alas, after only a short distance, a large furry animal attacked him. The animal played toyfully with his attempts at escape, but was distracted momentarily. This gave the individual a chance to dash back to the thick, green, protective cover of the jungle. The animal followed in close pursuit for a short distance but soon lost interest. Surely he was safe now. Not so—almost immediately a deluge of water drenched him from above. Miraculously the water stopped as quickly as it had started. He was wet to the bone but his spirits were not dampened. Surely now he could start his safe journey home, which he did.

He became jubilant as he neared the edge of the jungle and a sure path to safety. Then all of a sudden an enormous mechanical monster belching smoke and emitting a roaring-like sound began stalking him from behind, closing the distance rapidly. Cringing he hid behind a large boulder. Fortunately the mechanical monster noisily changed course and began tearing up the jungle in another direction. Surely the Lord was with him, he thought, heaving a sigh of gratitude.

Thud. Bump. Bump. Rumble. What was this rolling toward him now? It looked like the huge boulder in *Indiana Jones and the Raider of the Lost Ark*. The white, dimpled object resembled a giant snowball, ready to engulf him as it rolled towards him at breakneck speed.

In a moment of fear my friend took cover under a large umbrella-like plant. The round white object stopped just short of his tiny body. Burying itself in the matted floor of his green sanctuary.

Thump—thump—thump. What next? There on the horizon stood a giant, dressed in shorts and a funny little hat. The real scary part was the long skinny club he was grasping and waving in his hand. He headed in my friend's direction muttering to himself with each giant step. As my friend turned, fleeing in terror, he almost fell into a round cavernous hole. Oddly enough, this hole had a tall, numbered flag protruding from its center. By swerving to his left in a quick maneuver, he was able to avoid certain injury only by mere inches. You may be asking yourself by this time, what is going on here? The explanation is simple, although not all that obvious.

Problems like these are common if you are a large black beetle that lives on a golf course, which must be watered and mowed by groundskeepers. One that has a large furry cat for a club house pet and golfers like me who mutter and stare threateningly while trying to find a lost ball, hiding under a toadstool.

I was able to convince my friend the beetle to leave this dangerous environment by placing him in a small jar and taking him to a more secure place in the country, one that will still offer him daily challenge but with less threatening circumstances.

As in this tale of my friend the beetle, troublesome things in life are not always what they seem to be.

WORDS MAKE A DIFFERENCE

Every period of time brings about changes in the English language. Jargon that wasn't used six months ago becomes part of your daily conversation. Phrasessuch as *Spice Girls* do not refer to salt and pepper. The word *stress* has become almost as overused as the not so enduring term *relationship*.

To me, the word *stress* depicts something that is being stretched or pushed to its limits, even to the breaking point. In the past it was used more in reference to structural or material objects. In the last twenty years the term refers mostly to the physical and emotional well-being of humans. "I'm stressed or stressed out," have become buzzwords of the '80s through the '90s. This word has become the darling of every ad agency and law office in the country.

Imagine if you can, a crusty ol' army sergeant returning to his platoon after an overnight search-and-destroy mission. An extremely tense and emotional experience, as no one will deny. His eyes are burning from searching the inky darkness for hours looking for the enemy and he's physically and emotionally exhausted. He appears out of the darkness stumbling into his lighted bunker, throws his helmet to the ground and collapses next to two buddies. They turn to him and ask, "Are you ok?" He would probably answer, "I need some chow and about 10 hours of sleep, then I'll be fine." You certainly wouldn't hear the phase, "I'm stressed out."

My father didn't come home from work saying he was stressed. If he had I would have asked him in shocked surprise, "What happened, did you get hurt?" He would say he was tired and that was to be expected after a trying day—certainly nothing to indicate he had been stretched beyond his endurance. In actuality the word *stress* doesn't fit most human circumstances. Try using the words *tired, fatigued* or even *played out* instead of *stress*. You might even feel better for it and so will those around you,

Another word that has gone out of style is *love*. It has been replaced with the word *relationship*. The phrases, "I'm in a relationship" or "I'm having a relationship" are the phrases used by couples these days, not the word *love*. So I'm not surprised that divorce, separation, and couples living together without marriage has been the norm, not the exception. Sure, there are many underlying reasons and this may seem like an oversimplification. But my explanation holds some validity. After all, communication, liberally sprinkled with the word love, is the staff of life for a successful marriage.

Why isn't the word *love* used more often? Because the word *love* in itself spells commitment. When you say, "I love you" to someone, it means you will be there for better or worse. It means you will daily give of yourself to your partner. It means you are not afraid of the commitment of marriage. Love holds marriages together, not relationships. The word *relationship* intentionally excludes the commitment of love.

Love was never meant to be replaced by a buzzword. It is a lasting term of endearment that should be cradled and cherished by two people in love, not a relationship. Even the term *love affair* is more meaningful than the cold, stark term *relationship*. Most of history's most enduring love affairs would never have withstood only a relationship.

Relationship is that laidback noncommitted feeling that, oh well, if this one doesn't work out there will always be another and another, et cetera. Real bonding of a couple is never complete if the word *relationship* is used instead of *love*. Love personifies family, companionship and commitment that lasts a lifetime.

Next time you find yourself involved with the opposite sex, try using the word *love* in place of *relationship*. Surprisingly, you may find yourselves building a stronger foundation as a couple than any of your past experiences. The results will be assuredly more gratifying to you and your partner.

Remember, the word *relationship* will never hold the promise of love.

DEMONS OF THE ROAD

I felt assured all my ties with tanks and other mobile armored vehicles were severed when I left the army. My chances of being put in harm's way would be all part of my past. What a mistaken assumption this turned out to be.

Today I have seen a rebirth of these metal monsters in the form of SUVs, (sports utility vehicles). Their comrades-in-arms are those *huge* 4-wheel-drive pickups running on oversized tires, the kind that belong on earthmovers. Often you can't see through or around them because of their darkened windows. When one of these babies rumbles up behind you on a dark country road or anywhere for that matter, your vehicle will begin to shake, rattle, and roll. Sometimes your windshield washers even begin to weep. They usually stand from three to six feet taller than your form of transportation. With their halogen lights glaring like two monster eyes through your back window, your interior is transformed into a large-lighted ballroom. Unfortunately, you're trying to drive, not dance. After you narrowly avoid going off the road due to its seemingly hot breath breathing down your trunk, you regain your senses.

It won't be long before this piece of pseudo equipment from the

First Armored Division will pass you at 60 to 70 miles-per-hour, belching fire and smoke, almost sucking you up its tailpipe. You swear the driver is wearing combat fatigues, complete with helmet. Or is it a cowboy hat? Whatever, you throw them a salute as they pass, if you know what I mean.

The sad part is you don't need combat training to drive one of these piles of metal. Only a driver's license and the ability to reach the gas pedal, and sometimes I question the part about the license. Being able to reach the brake is strictly optional.

I'm glad teenagers can't afford these rigs. The large vibrating stereo systems they could hold would be enough to deafen everyone at a stop sign and for blocks around. When they take Dad's pride and joy on a Saturday night, besides the car key they also need one to Fort Knox so they can buy the gas.

When you see the price on these vehicles you realize the design engineers had the Midas touch. If you own one of these miniature buses your days of traveling coach class are over. Practicality is nowhere mentioned in Madison Avenue's ad copy in their quest to woo prospective buyers.

God only knows what they will be driving fifty years from now. I won't know because I undoubtedly will fall victim to one of these overindulgences of automotive engineering, a perfect monument to the human ego.

Good luck to you in all your encounters with these steel demons. Personally, I'll keep my Dodge Dart.

CLASS ACTION

Recently I attended my 47th class reunion. I had been bombarded with preregistration information for this event in January. I dutifully filed it under "Maybe I'll go, maybe I won't."

On the eve of the big event, I decided to go. After all, I hadn't seen most of my school friends since graduation. When we graduated it was like the novel "The Winds of War." Most of the males were drafted and the girls began working. Many never returned; some settled in far away places and some were lost in Korea.

Another strong reason for my attendance was the fact that I love to dance. I felt sure none of my old girlfriends would turn down "old twinkle toes" (a nickname I acquired as a senior), if I asked them to dance.

I hadn't been to a reunion in 25 years and I have been single for 23 of those years. What I have missed most being single is the companionship, pillow talk, and the feeling of intimacy that comes from sharing your love or tender touches with someone through years of togetherness. It takes a great deal of adjustment to go from a wife and four children to an empty apartment, but adjust you must.

Across the room stood Russ, one of my closest friends in high school and college. As I walked over, he extended his hand as we both said in unison, "Great to see you." His wife, Jan, was standing at his side looking as pretty as ever, a tinge of gray in her blond hair giving just a hint of the passing years. She smiled at me saying, "Jim, you haven't changed a bit." I grinned at this statement beneath a shock of snow white hair, thinking "Yeah right."

There were Lyle and Carol Ann; he looked fit and trim and Carol Ann was as pretty as ever. The only thing lacking was his football uniform and her cheerleading outfit.

"Hi, Sara, golly it's great to see you. You did a fantastic job on the committee.

"Louie, you remember that time we went hunting and you didn't have any boots, only Oxfords? It rained and snowed for two days." Louie just looked up at me and smiled.

And so it went as we reminisced throughout the evening.

The ticket included dinner; I wondered where I would sit as I entered the room. This question was quickly answered as I was hailed by Phyllis and Joanne, two women I hadn't seen since my last reunion. After introductions to their respective husbands, I took a seat and ordered the salmon. It was delicious and made so much more palatable by the conversation. We laughed as we talked about friends, past weenie roasts, firesides, football games, and the dances we had attended.

After the meal, I was waiting for the music to start when I felt a gentle squeeze on the back of my shoulder and heard the words, "Jim, is that you?" There she was, Joy! She looked just like she did on our last date, a wonderful dancing cruise on a summer moonlit night forty-seven years ago. I didn't have to glance at her nametag as I gave her a warm hug. "It's great to see you, Joy." I exclaimed. She looked up at me with the warm look I remembered so well. The look turned to pleasant laughter and she said, "I was hoping you'd be here. I want you to meet my new husband." I hesitated just a moment sinceI had heard she was single. I had lost again. We walked to their table where introductions and pleasantries were exchanged.

Shortly, I walked away a little befuddled. After all, at one time she had meant a great deal to me.

We danced later and I said, "It's like old times." She looked up with a smile and said, "You dumped me once, remember?" All I said was "What a mistake that was." I held her just a little tighter as I knew she'd walk away once more after this last dance.

The evening was drawing to a close as I watched my friends head out the door, most of them with wives and husbands, many with new mates. But there were still enough high school sweethearts holding hands as they departed into the night, enough of them for me to know that love can and does survive.

I grabbed my coat and a dose of reality and headed for my '67 Dodge Dart, glad I had come and vowing not to miss the next one, God willing. I made a quick stop at McDonalds for coffee and a hamburger, not because I was hungry but it just seemed like the right thing to do, sort of a fitting end to the evening. As I sat in my booth at this late hour I watched the high school couples come and go holding hands after a date. I thought to myself, most, if not all, of these kids will attend their forty-seventh year class reunion some day. Hopefully, with a little luck and perseverance they won't be going home alone. Perhaps my time is yet to come.

AN ANSWER TO PRAYER

My daughter Lori, fully clothed in winter attire, was preparing to go outside with Clancy, one of her two black labs. She had bundled up against the chilly springlike weather so she and Clancy could go out for their Sunday evening walk. She had promised him that morning if the rain stopped they would take a stroll down by the creek, his favorite destination.

Clancy, a black lab, and Lori, a spunky young woman, live in the country, near Spokane, Washington. Normally she lives alone with her horses and other pets. But at this particular point in time she had a roommate named Kristina. They were friends and Kristina was there to help defray expenses. Lori was going to college and working only part-time. She had been a vet technician but was now going for a career as a registered dietician.

The expression, "Where were you when I needed you?" would not hold water in Clancy's and Duke's, Lori's other Lab's case. For time and time again, they had been there for her.

They were there when the knocks came at her door in the dark of night, far from any neighbors. With their incessant barking and growls, the knocks didn't last long. When the neighborhood ruffian from up the road decided to climb up a tree to peep into Lori's bedroom, he learned firsthand that Clancy certainly was not his best friend.

All he left behind was his telltale baseball cap beneath the tree, dropped as he scampered for home with Clancy on his heels. He never returned.

Duke was Lori's first lab. She taught him to retrieve but would not allow him to hunt, much to my chagrin. His confidence and constant alertness always allowed her to sleep soundly at night. Clancy came several years later to join Duke, adding his deep growl and benevolent character.

Twice daily, in the cold winter morning darkness and again in the darkness of winter evenings, she fed her horses and Toughie, the yellow barn cat. This meant a long trek through deep snow.

As she trudged knee-deep in the snow toward the barn, Duke and Clancy eased her loneliness with their comical actions, bounding and barking between mouthfuls of snow. Their playful shenanigans left her no time to think of the darkness and what it could hold. Besides, Toughie the barn cat was there waiting to be fed. Mouse hunting was lean in the winter. Before they left the barn, Toughie always gave Clancy and Duke's curious noses a quick, gentle tap or two, just to remind them who really ruled the barn.

For their unselfish loyalty, unequivocal love, and companionship, Clancy and Duke expected nothing in return but a pat on their heads and Lori's praising soft voice, plus a dish of dog chow. Oh yes, and on really cold days, an extra treat would be forthcoming. They also shared some of their mistress's piping hot cereal. Even though they were mannerly, they were always done before she ever got hers cool enough to eat.

In summer the gentle tugs and nips they bestowed upon her swimsuit while they all three swam in the cold creek nearby were cheerfully accepted. She knew they were nothing but a gentle reminder that her two strong swimming companions were there if needed.

On one occasion I watched as Clancy and Duke came face to face with a pack of coyotes that had invaded the horse corral where a new foal was standing. This led to a hair-raising barking and posturing standoff for quite some time, but goodness finally prevailed and the pack dispersed.

Lori's relationship with Clancy became stronger when Duke developed arthritis. He is now gray-faced and can no longer take part in all their activities, such as playing stick or taking long walks. Too many winters and ensuing trips through the deep snow to feed have taken their toll. Those swims in the icy creek didn't help either.

Getting back to my story. When Lori finished her chores in the house she looked out the kitchen window and noticed it had quit raining, something it hadn't done for several days. It was time to take Clancy for his promised walk, she thought to herself as she pulled on her down-filled jacket and laced up her heavy boots, which she would wish later that she hadn't worn—but I'm getting ahead of my story.

Clancy, along with Duke, was lying on the back porch, sleeping bundles of black lab, love and loyalty. Lori nudged Clancy gently as she passed and spoke enthusiastically, "Come, Clancy, we're going for a walk before it gets too dark." Needless to say ol' Clancy only had to be asked once. He almost knocked her down in his effort to get out the door before her. She smiled at his joyful enthusiasm. Duke gave them a lab smile but remained on the porch since his arthritis was acting up. He would wait for warmer weather.

Lori and Clancy started their walk along the road in the direction of the nearby creek. Before they had gone only a short distance, black clouds began to roll in and darken the sky. Once more it began to spit rain. "Oh no," she thought, "more rain we really don't need."

She yelled at Clancy, who had bounded ahead of her and had reached the bridge that crossed the creek. "Come on, Clancy, we have to head for home." Clancy, busy chasing a mouse, paid her no mind. He didn't mind the rain and besides he hadn't had a swim in months and here he was at the creek.

Lori, losing patience by the minute, yelled again, "Come on, Clancy, we have to head home, no swim for you today." But no one told Clancy. With his head up in a graceful leap he left the bridge and entered the tumultuous water.

Unbeknownst to them both, the stream had become a torrent, almost overnight, due to the rapid runoff of rain and melting snow in the nearby mountains. Under normal circumstances his dive into the stream would have held no consequences for this strong swimming lab. But these were not normal circumstances.

A barbed-wire fence that surrounded the pasture crossed the creek at this juncture also. Normally the fence would be at least two feet above the flowing water but due to the extremely high water it was now flowing through the fence. In no time at all Clancy was in deep water and in serious trouble.

In a matter of seconds the force of the water swept him solidly up against the fence. He struggled to swim towards shore to no avail. The more he struggled the more entangled he became. Lori had seen his leap from the bridge and when he didn't appear on the opposite bank she became concerned. She hurried towards the bridge calling his name all the way. "Yes," she thought, "Clancy, you're in big trouble." How right she was and without realizing it.

When she reached the bridge she was met by a frightening sight. Clancy was impaled against the barbwire fence, struggling and whimpering in desperation, trying to free himself. Lori took one look at this frightful scene and instantly realized he needed help at once.

Without hesitation she jumped into the swift-flowing stream, failing to remove her heavy boots or down jacket. They immediately began to pull her down in the deep icy water, leaving her gasping for breath. In a matter of seconds she also was impaled on the fence next to a struggling Clancy. She grabbed him and held his head up with one hand and grasped the wire with her other hand. For the moment they were safe.

With the frigid water draining her strength Lori told me later she knew she had to make a decision, either let go of Clancy or hold on and risk both of them drowning. "I can't let go of Clancy, God," she prayed, "But I can't hold on much longer. *Please,* I need your help!"

She knew they had to get out of the freezing water before hypothermia set in. She related to me later that at this moment in time she started to pray and asked God for help. Like a miracle, on the usually deserted road a pickup truck appeared. The driver, with his eyes on the road would never see them, Lori thought. At this time Lori prayed once more, "Dear God, please help us."

The truck neared and crossed the bridge causing Lori's heart to drop. Then almost like an answer to Lori's prayers it stopped and backed up on the bridge. Two men emerged from the truck and in seconds the two ran down the embankment, yelling, "Hold on there! We'll be right down." One grabbed the fence and reached out his hand. New strength surged through Lori as she swung Clancy over so the man could reach him. He grabbed the dog, then passed him up the bank to his buddy. Then he reached out once again, this time for Lori. She was able to give him a free hand and he pulled her out of the water, boots and all.

On the way back to the ranch Lori asked the rescuer, "How did you ever see me in the water?" "I really don't know," he said. "We just decided to take this road instead of our usual route. As we were talking, I happened to glance out my window, and I saw your blonde head above the murky water—lucky you." But Lori knew deep in her heart it wasn't luck that stopped the truck on the deserted road— it was God.

After arriving back at the ranch Lori and Clancy walked through the back door. Kristina, waiting in the doorway, took one look at Lori's wet, shuddering, disheveled appearance and asked in alarm. "What happened to you?" With tears running down her already wet face, an emotionally and physically exhausted Lori looked up at Kristina and in a quivering voice, said through chattering teeth, "Kristina, God does answer prayers."

RUSTY'S WINDOW

My name is Rusty, because of my bright, shiny, orange and white coat. I'm a neutered male cat of mixed origins, with a great personality. I live on a ranch, in rolling hill country in the great northwest.

My owner and friend is named Lori. She is a single lady, thirty-nine years of age, and has she got spunk. She rises every morning in the wintertime and feeds five horses in below-freezing weather. She also feeds Clancy and Duke, her two black labs who just happen to be friends of mine. She does all of this before she rushes off to a large hospital to work as a registered dietician. While she is away I spend many hours in my picture window watching all the beauty of the surrounding countryside and waiting patiently for her return.

Sometimes a bird will perch on the flowerbox outside my window causing me to make strange noises in my throat and my body to shudder with excitement. This makes me realize I still have my natural hunting instincts. The quick, comical movements of the chipmunks, who come to feed on seeds placed on my windowsill, make me grin like a Cheshire cat.

Occasionally I sneak out when Lori isn't looking, but she always comes and catches me. I really don't mind because I know she is doing it for my own good. She has lost other cats to traffic and lurking coyotes. Besides, I want to sit in my picture window for years to come and she makes this possible. When she arrives home from work I greet her at the door for I have seen her coming. She has a warm, friendly greeting for me as she gently strokes my purring body. If I'm lucky she will give me a treat before dinner. She has taught me manners, so I do not beg. I just coyly brush against her legs and it works every time. When she leans over with my treat I daintily take it from her outstretched hand. She then smiles and says, "Rusty, you have such good manners." Yes, there is such a thing as cat smoozing, meow!

After she completes her busy evening of dinner, laundry, and other home chores, she goes out to the horses and spends time with them. Stormy, her year-old filly, so named because she was born on a dark and stormy night, gets the most attention. It has been fun watching Stormy grow and develop from my perch in the window. She and Lori are already great pals. I can see and feel their bonding as Stormy nickers and nuzzles Lori's blond head. It will be fun to watch her break and train this bay-colored, spirited animal. I have often watched Stormy race through the tall grass in the pasture, throwing her head up and down and side to side, her copper-colored mana glistening in the sun. She ends her sprint with her head pointed towards the sky and a joyful whinny, like she is glad to be alive.

One Saturday afternoon as the wind and the rain beat heavily against my window, I came up with a plan. When the weather cleared I would sneak outside. Lori would be busy all afternoon cleaning the barn and working with the horses.

If I waited long and quietly enough in the darkened corner of the porch, I'd be able to sneak out before the screen door slammed shut, as Lori went outside. I have practiced this trick before but Lori was always able to grab me just as I darted between her legs. This time I would until she went through the door, jump out and turn immediately to my left. She would never see me.

It has been so long since I have been outside mouse hunting. I really long for such an adventure. Besides I don't want to lose my hunting skills. Who knows when I may really need them?

As I waited in the dark corner I heard Lori approaching the screen door. Here was my chance, whoosh, I just made it and she didn't even see me. Although I felt a little guilty for a fleeting second, the feeling soon passed. With pure joy I bounded through the short wheat stubble near the house. Surely there would be a mouse or two hiding in the short golden stalks. Within minutes I spotted a little wee gray one as it unsuspectingly chewed on a kernel of wheat lying on the ground.

Here was my chance. As I shivered with excitement, I started my stalk. Yes, I would have a prize to present to Lori when I returned home. With such a trophy she would surely forgive me for my adventure outside the safety of our home.

Slowly, I put one foot in front of the other and quietly approached the feeding mouse. Then I began to feel uneasy. Everything was perfect. What could possibly be going wrong? Something warned me to look behind and then I saw it—a coyote not three feet away, stalking me. I wheeled and started to run for the house in great bounding leaps. Please God, I prayed, let me make it to the tree in the backyard. I promise if you do I will never leave the safety of the house again. The coyote was gaining ground rapidly but the tree was also getting closer with each of my giant leaps. I was going to make it, I gasped, and with one final leap I felt the tree bark beneath my sharp claws. I'd made it. Perched high above my attacker, on a limb, I sighed with relief. It wasn't long before the coyote lost interest in me and trotted back into the wheat stubble. Just before he disappeared he turned and gave me a frightening look. From the safety of the tree I again counted my blessings. I decided then, I would never leave the house again. I owe you one, God.

As I sat quietly on the limb wondering if I should try for the house I heard Lori's soft voice. "So that's where you are, Rusty. I have been looking all over for you. Don't you know that there are coyotes out here and you could end up as someone's dinner?" Boy, did I ever know what she was talking about.

She gently reached up to my purring body and lifted me from the safety of my perch. I clung softly to her neck as we started towards the house, with all its warmth and comfort. Yes, I had learned a big lesson today. I would never again disobey Lori. After all, I wanted to sit in my window once again. The soft warm comforter on the bed would feel extra special tonight. Old Mr. Coyote is disappointed and probably a little bit hungry. Thanks, Lori.

It was the morning after my adventure. I had not slept well the previous night, even though I had snuggled as close to Lori as possible. It would be a while before my heartbeat returned to normal.

Later in the morning, I took my usual seat in the window and began to doze and dream. Before I knew it, in my dream I was in full pursuit of Ol' Mr. Coyote. Now he was bounding through the stubble with me close on his heels. I almost had him but he reached his den and bolted down the dark hole in the ground. Lost him, darn it! Surprise—within moments he was back outside with a badger snapping at his backside. I smiled to myself. Now it's your turn Mr. Coyote. About this time I woke up and knew everything was now ok.

Spring, summer and fall are fairly easy as the horses are in the pasture. Wintertime is different. When you are no bigger than a minute and have to buck hay bales into a feeding rack, it's a tough job. But I never hear her complain as she comes into the house stomping the snow from her boots. Her clothes always have that fresh smell of cold air about them. Hopefully, she will put some in the laundry basket so I can have another cozy place to catnap.

At night when I yawn and stretch full length till my legs quiver, I know it's time for bed. I like this time best because that's when Lori and I retire to a very large old-fashioned brass bed for our night's sleep. It has the warmest, most elegant comforter on it that you can ever imagine and I get to sleep at the foot near a shiny brass rail. Sometimes when she is asleep I get lonely and sneak up close to her and she really doesn't mind.

Often when it's late at night and the moon is full and bright, with moonbeams dancing on the walls, I hear the coyotes howling. When this occurs, I just snuggle closer to Lori, for I know in my own heart that thanks to her I will be able to sit in my picture window tomorrow and watch the world go by. Maybe a chipmunk will stop by and make me grin.

BEST FRIENDS

For years, and even longer than that, the expression *man's best friend* has been bantered about in our language with great abandon. If the truth were known this phrase in reference to dogs is not entirely accurate. And in this age of political correctness this misnomer should be corrected.

Exceptional bonding between dogs and members of the female gender also exists and in many instances is even stronger. A dog's protective instinct seems to be keener when a gentler, smaller master is involved, like a woman or child. They seem to sense these individuals need special attention. Very often we hear of heroic acts by dogs in defense of children or their female masters. I know of two dogs that fit this profile, Duke and Clancy.

To many on the prairie where these two live they are known as the mischievous duo, as they are seldom apart. No serious trouble, you understand, just two pals out having fun and getting into a little mischief now and then. But in reality they are love, loyalty, and protection, all wrapped in the tail-wagging bodies of black labradors.

A spunky young woman who prefers to live in the country alone with her horses and other pets is their mistress. The expression, "Where were you when I needed you?" would not hold water in Duke's and Clancy's case. For time and time again they have always been there for her.

They were there when the knocks came at her door in the dark of night, far from any neighbors. With their incessant barking and growls the knocks never lasted long.

When the neighborhood ruffian from up the road decided to climb up a tree to peep into the young woman's bedroom, he learned firsthand that Clancy certainly was not his best friend. All he left behind was his telltale baseball hat beneath the tree. It was dropped as he scampered for home with Clancy on his heels. He never returned.

Duke was her first Lab. She taught him to retrieve but would not allow him to hunt, much to my chagrin. His confidence and constant alertness always allowed her to sleep soundly at night. Clancy came several years later to join Duke and added his deep growl and benevolent character.

Twice daily, in the cold winter-morning darkness and again in the early darkness of winter evenings she fed her horses and the yellow barn cat Toughie. This meant a long trek through deep snow. As she trudged knee-deep in the snow towards the barn Duke and Clancy eased her loneliness with their comical actions, bounding and barking between grabbing mouthfuls of snow. Their playful shenanigans left her no time to think of the darkness and what it could hold. Besides, Toughie would be there waiting to be fed. Mouse hunting was lean in the winter. Before they left, Toughie gave Duke and Clancy's curious noses a quick gentle tap or two, just to remind them who really ruled the barn.

For their unselfish loyalty and companionship Duke and Clancy expected nothing in return but a pat on their heads and her praising soft voice plus a dish of dog chow. Oh yes, and on really cold days an extra treat would be forthcoming. They got to share some of their mistress' piping hot cereal. Even though they were mannerly, they were always done before she ever got hers blown cool. That was ok, for there would be more the next morning.

In summer the gentle tugs and nips that they bestowed upon her swimsuit while they all three swam in the cold nearby creek were cheerfully accepted. She knew they were nothing but a gentle reminder that her two strong swimming companions were there if needed.

When a new foal arrived these two took it upon themselves to make sure it wasn't harmed, although it always was difficult to convince the mare and foal they meant no harm. Cocking their heads, they would watch their newfound friend struggle to gain its footing on long, gangly legs. Its wobbly legs were not quite sure just which way to go. While Duke and Clancy sat on their haunches, like a cheering section, the foal finally stood. The mare allowed their nearness since she sensed the pair meant no harm. These two were always great con artists.

It was no time at all until a bond was formed and the mischievous duo had another charge to protect and protect, they did. On one occasion I watched as they both came face to face with a pack of coyotes who had invaded the foal's corral. This led to a hair-raising, barking, and posturing standoff for quite some time but goodness finally prevailed and the pack dispersed. Man's best friend—hardly in this case.

Duke and Clancy's job is coming to a close since their mistress has found another protector in a husband. She recently married. Just in time I'd say, as Duke is now gray-faced and crippled up with arthritis. Too many winters and ensuing trips through deep snow to feed. All those swims in the icy creek didn't help either.

Clancy left us only a few months ago, but everyone agrees he's got a new job in heaven. He was put in charge of protection and affection for "The Littlest Angel." In this scenario he has become an angel's best friend.

The next time you hear or use the expression *man's best friend*, you can smile to yourself because you know better. A dog is not just man's best friend. A dog is just a friend, period.

WINTER'S LIGHT IS SPECIAL

Surprisingly, the sight that reminds me most of winter is not leaves turning golden and falling to the ground. It's not the chill in the air as night approaches and the days grow short. It's not even the light wisps of snow mixed with rain. It's the color of the sky and surrounding area as evening approaches and at sunrise. It's that blue-pink color that turns to a purple glow all around us. When this starts, you know winter is here.

No other season produces this aura. My memories are always stirred by it. A picture of an outdoor skating rink comes to mind, along with crackling bonfires, warm sweaters and sweatshirts. I look forward to that cozy feeling of cotton fleece next to my skin. Laughter echoes through the sharp winter air as children play and shuffle in large mounds of fallen leaves. This always brings a smile to my face. An odor of cold air lingers on my clothes as I step inside my home, never forgetting to stomp my feet free from the messy wet snow. The smell and sight of wood smoke as it curls from chimneys throughout the neighborhood completes this Norman Rockwell winter scene in my mind.

Most of all it reminds me of families gathered around a fireplace, engaged in lively conversation and the feeling of love as you tuck the little ones in at the end of the day, their faces flushed the color of red roses from the crisp outdoor air.

These memories and visions are not enjoyed by the inhabitants of warmer climates. I feel sorry for them and don't envy their year-round temperatures.

I just looked out the window and saw a mule deer doe and yearling, belly-deep in snow. They were unconcerned but the excitement they caused in our house was something to see and hear. The grandchildren pressed their faces to the window and chattered excitedly as they viewed this winter mural created by Mother Nature. Moments like these are always more memorable when shared with a child, especially a grandchild, an extension of your own life.

Yes, the color of the sky does affect your mood. I always await the purple glow of winter evenings with great anticipation. Perhaps it will add another memory to my life, like the doe and fawn belly, deep in snow, as seen from the front room window, with that purple aura all around them.

SKIPPING GRANDPARENT

Have any of you grandparents out there tried skipping recently? No, I'm not talking about skipping school, skipping work, or skipping a meal. I'm talking about old-fashioned skipping down the street. One foot in front of the other in a hip-hop fashion, remember? It's a childhood pleasure that you never forget—just like riding a bike.

Let me tell you about my grandfatherly experience. A little blonde girl with long curls was walking with her mother in front of me. All of a sudden she broke into laughter and began to skip. Her mother smiled and said, "Slow down, Cindy, and watch out for cars." I couldn't help myself and I wasn't going to let my sixty-seven years stop me. With a smile and white hair flying, I skipped right past her mother and soon passed the little girl. "Hey, Grandpa," she called after me, "slow down or you will have a heart attack." Fat chance, I thought, no one has a heart attack when they are having fun. Her mom, in a scolding voice said, "Cindy, shame on you. Show some respect for your elders."

With each skip, joy swelled within me. After a half block I slowed down but not before I called back to the little girl—"It's like riding a bike, you never forget."

Why do we forget the little joys of childhood as we get older? To refresh your memory, try an afternoon nap on a sunny park bench, with birds singing and children laughing in the background. These sounds flowing together in a musical summer overture create a concert of memories.

A good Saturday matinee with a big orange and a bag of popcorn will do more for the spirit than any tranquilizer prescribed by your doctor. Age has no barriers in a theater except for the price of admission. You can't even squat down and say, "One child, please" anymore. The twinkle is still in your eyes but so are the age lines around their corners. Oh well, you can still enjoy the movie. It's like riding a bike; you never forget those past Saturday matinees.

How do you get from skipping to downhill skiing? It's easy, rent a pair of skis, grab a boda bag of hot-spiced wine, and jump on the chair lift. You did it forty years ago and you can still do it. It's like riding a bike, you never forget. I don't care if you are a grandparent.

A pickup game of basketball with the "old gang" is a lot like skipping when it comes to fun. As you race up and down the court tossing the ball here and there you suddenly spot your best shooter open in the 3-point zone. With a behind-the-back pass that would do Michael Jordan proud a perfect pass is made. Swoosh, he made it, nothing but net. It's just like riding a bike, you never forget, as long as you practice with the "old gang" once in a while.

Who said tennis was a sissy sport? The pretty girl standing all alone next to the tennis court entrance didn't think you had forgotten how to serve when she asked, "Would you like to play a couple of sets?" Don't hesitate, remember, it's like riding a bike, you never forget. If you do, who really cares? She certainly didn't.

Standing next to the pool at the YMCA you begin to shiver just a little. Your boxer shorts bathing suit, clinging precariously around your tiny protruding belly, looks woefully out of place amid all the Speedo's but hopefully no one will notice. About this time your young grandson runs by and says, "I'll race you to the end of the pool, Grandpa." You're startled but game, as you bellyflop into the pool; you never were good at diving. Halfway down the pool, as you struggle with your Australian crawl, a smile comes to your face amid the bubbles—yup, it's just like riding a bike, you never forget. You only forget that you're old enough to be a white-haired grandparent.

On the way home from each of these excursions you feel warm inside. Sure you will be a little bit stiff in the morning but after all, you proved something to yourself, after each one of your physical escapades—each of life's experiences is like riding a bicycle, you never forget the fun ones, hopefully only the unpleasant ones.

All these thoughts are running through your mind as you skip down the street with the little girl close behind and gaining slowly. After all, it's easy to dream sweet dreams and skip at the same time. That's why skippers are always smiling, just like the little blonde girl with long curls. It's easy, just like riding a bike, and don't you ever forget it—even if you are a grandparent.

CASTING A LONG SHADOW

It was always an extremely busy place. The background rumbling and hissing outside its doors added to the turmoil. Redcaps pushing and carrying baggage here and there were also part of the bustling atmosphere. Loudspeakers blaring names of places I had never been to but hopefully would see some day, completed the scene.

This beautiful brick building had lots of windows. It was almost hidden among all the old warehouses, loading docks, and trestles, in an area commonly called skid row. More often than not on sunny weekends transients could be seen sleeping in the nearby warehouse doorways and on the loading docks. It certainly wasn't surrounded by lush green manicured lawns, being enjoyed by space-conscious urbanites as well as those from the suburbs.

The river that ran close by wasn't clean and sparkling as it is now. For years its waters had been filled with the city's waste. Ducks and geese, engaging in their ceaseless social chatter, were seldom seen riding its swift current and swans were unheard of. Yes, this was the setting of the old Great Northern Train Depot. Now all that remains of the depot structure is its noble-looking clock tower, standing so grand in Riverfront Park. Most couples strolling hand in hand on the nearby walkways have no idea of its treasured past. Unknownst to them Harry (Bing) Lillis Crosby, along with others, had penned his name near its mechanism years before when he worked there as a young man—a fact related to me by retired station supervisor Harry Wihl Borg.

Frisbees are tossed between boys and girls in a rhythmic fashion. Small children run across the lush green meadowlike grass. Some small ones are practicing their rolling ability on one of the park's steep hills. Moms are heard scolding, "Get up, you will get grass stains on your clothes." Laughing, the small ones stand up but will be rolling again as soon as the moms turn their backs. After all, isn't that what the soft grass is for?

Seems like most strollers end up at the popcorn or hot dog wagon for a cool drink and a snack. Some can be seen enjoying a picnic lunch beneath the willows that line the shady, gentle banks along the river. Pets are leashed and usually well behaved. I have been told that boys bring their pets to the park for more than exercise. They have found they are an excellent conversation starter with the opposite sex. The smart ones adorn their pet's necks with a bright bandana that will bring a smile to some pretty girl's face, and go from there. Sounds perfectly reasonable to me. Towering above this tranquil parklike scene is the imposing clock tower. This tall, inescapable remnant of Spokane's past casts an eerie shadow across the park's lush, manicured meadows.

I took only one trip out of this architectural beauty, designed mostly for practicality with only its imposing tower looking out of the ordinary. Seems like everyone who entered through its doors was interested in only one thing, getting to where they were going. No one had time to view a waterfall or sculptured bronze figures. Who could ever imagine a walkway to its entrance, framed by tall, ominous stone pillars? I had visited it many times to pick up and deliver friends and relatives and, like most, was always impressed.

My one trip out of the old depot was to Fort Ord, California, in the early '50s. I was headed for basic training in the U.S. Army. The usual tears were shed by family and friends but in a way I was excited. Everything is exciting when you're twenty-two years old and feeling invincible. I had just graduated from college and become engaged; I had the world by the tail and nothing could stop me now. Even so, I was only one of thousands over the years who left this station with some uncertainty in their hearts. Train stations, airports, and bus depots all seem to generate this fleeting feeling.

It started me on an adventure that will never be duplicated and is, in some ways better forgotten. Like many others, I returned to the station once again. Thousands of miles had passed beneath my boots and the emotional highs and lows were far too many to chronicle.

These are the thoughts I have as I stand quietly and view the clock tower in Riverfront Park. The station is gone but the stately tower remains standing like a lonely sentinel. The river is clean now and reflects its new purity in the bright sunlight. The ducks, geese and swans, preening and diving, seem so content as they glide past the tower's shadow in perfect formation, adding to the tranquil setting. They know someone will throw them treats from their picnic basket if they get close to shore. Laughing voices echo across the river as bold ducks eat from children's tiny hands, tickling them in the process.

There are other attractions in Riverfront Park that reflect the personality of the city. The Red Wagon is adored by young children and adults alike. The arcade and Imax are also much appreciated. The Vietnam Veterans Monument brings a peaceful, warm solace to many. Everyone enjoys the fairyland-like carousel with its melodic music and laughing riders astride prancing horses. This nostalgic bit of Spokane is another story all in itself.

Yet none are so meaningful to most as the striking clock tower. The old depot tower holds different memories for everyone but most importantly it's a link to the past. What memories, if any, does it hold for you? All fond ones, I hope.

TRAPPED BY YOUR CELL

We recently stepped into the twenty-first century but in reality we are stepping back into the nineteenthentury. You may think this is not possible but believe me, it is. The next time you see your neighbors leave their homes, cell phones in hand, picture their cells—short for cell phones—as their trusty muskets—their dapper work suits as buckskins.

Only they won't have their Kentucky long rifles in hand, just their cell phones. Their belts contains pagers that look like ammunition holders and holster for their cells. All within easy reach for a quick draw—ring, ring.

Although I don't feel the holster is necessary, since most of the time the cells never leave their hands till they go to bed and I'm not so sure they release it then. Now the cell is not really a lethal weapon but I'm sure many of us have felt talked to death by the holder of one, at one time or another.

There is one case where the cell should be considered dangerous. Just put one in the hands of a driver behind the wheel of a monstrous SUV (sport utility vehicle) or any vehicle and forget to take away his or her calling card. The devastation wreaked in heavy traffic on a freeway is a horrible sight to see. As the victim is pried from the wreckage, cell in hand, it's stuck to their ear and a smile is on their face.

The only sound you hear will be moaning and groaning from the injured, and a tiny voice repeating over and over: "If you have a call to make please hang up and place your call again." I don't think so.

There is a birth defect that will come about in the new millennium and medical science is desperately trying to come up with a solution. Unfortunately at this time they still haven't found a cure for babies who will be born with a cell in hand. They are hoping to find something in generic medicine to combat this birth defect. They are working on the theory that parents with unlisted numbers have a better chance of having a normal child.

Soon telephone companies will usher in ad campaigns extolling the benefits of unlisted numbers. It will be only one of many services provided by these communications giants. If they have their way your phone bill will soon be higher than your mortgage payments if it isn't already.

The cell has many advantages over a pistol or long rifle. It has a much longer range, is lighter in weight, and in a real desperate situation you can put your attacker on hold, or call waiting. I knew there must be a need somewhere for call waiting, other than just being a rude moneymaker for the phone company.

I realize there are pros and cons over which cell to purchase. All phone companies have their own marketing ploys, just like the gun makers of yesteryear. There is only one difference. When you purchased your trusty musket or pistol you bought and paid for it at the time of purchase. Not so with the cell. You will be saddled, and I'm not talking about your horse, with feeding its voracious appetite for the rest of your days. It is best to use these cell weapons only after 5 PM because ammunition is cheaper. Just remember your bill goes on and on just like the memory bank on your phone.

I can't imagine anyone so bold as to leave home without their cell in the twenty-first century. It will simply not be safe. We outgrew the musket but have reverted to packing a pistol in many urban areas. None of these weapons are as sophisticated as a cell, however. Besides, you don't need a background check to purchase one, although background checks may be needed in the future. Woe unto the individual who has left an unpaid phone bill in their dark and distant past. No cell phone for you.

Cell phones have been known to suck common sense from the user's brain. Why else would someone going 70 miles per hour call home, ask for the grocery list, and attempt to write it down, all the while negotiating the freeway off-ramp.

The cell can be a mom's worst nightmare when she heads out the door for some quiet time to herself. Then all at once Dad's and the kids' voices, sounding like an anvil chorus, follow her out the door. "Don't forget your cell, Mom, we may need to get hold of you." — Count on it. Dads hear the music too. Do yourself and everyone around you a favor. Face the friendly world today unarmed. Leave the cell at home. It can be done.

I was never concerned about Y2K but I am concerned about the cell and you should be too. I swear the other day I saw a baby strapped in a car seat w-a-a-a-y in the back of as SUV—phone in hand. Mom, w-a-a-a-y up in the front seat, weaving in and out of traffic, also has her cell in hand. You don't suppose baby was telling mom she needed a diaper change, do you?

Maybe the baby doesn't need a change but we do. Let's go back to the musket and cap and ball pistol. They were safer, cheaper, and didn't make as much noise in a crowded public place. Ring—ring—ring.

IT WASN'T JUST A
QUESTION OF PREGNANCY

The soctor sitting directly across from my wife and me spoke with a smile and gentle authority, "There is no question, you two, Lois is pregnant." Boy, would he be wrong on this statement, I realized later. Not on the pregnancy, but on the question part.

I was sleeping soundly when out of the blue I was rudely awakened by a tender nudge. "Jim, are you awake?" my wife, Lois, asked softly. "I am now." I said, with just a touch of displeasure in my voice. After all she wasn't sleeping much either.

Since Lois was seven months pregnant I had become accustomed to these late-night interruptions in my sleep cycle. All of these middle-of-the-night conversation encounters were necessary, I realized, and I took them in stride—certainly not in my sleep.

I had been awakened with questions like, "Jim, would you get me a glass of water?" "Jim, would you please stop snoring, I can't sleep?" "Jim, what do you think we should name the baby if it's a girl?" "Jim, what do you think we should name the baby if it's a boy?" "Jim, would you make me a sandwich?" These are just a few of these very necessary, important questions I was telling you about.

As the pregnancy grew in length, my sleep grew less and less. Like the night I was brought out of a sound sleep with this startling remark, "Jim, put your hand here on my stomach and feel the baby. It's kicking me."

Now I don't want you to think I was uninterested, but my God, it was 3 AM and I had to go to work in the morning. Click, on came the light and with doctor-like tenderness I began to check out our future bundle of joy's calisthenics. He—perhaps this was wishful thinking— was playing in Mom's soft, warm gym and he didn't have to pay any monthly dues. I laughed at baby's budget plan. I guess if the baby couldn't sleep it didn't expect us to either. This attitude would linger even after birth as we both would find out at 3 AM feeding time.

My wife enjoyed all the fun parts of pregnancy. This included baby showers, baby shopping sprees with her pregnant friends, and little coffee klatches in the late morning after sleeping in. These gatherings always included lots of tiny desserts. What is it they say? "Birds of a feather flock together," or in this case, "Expectant mothers eat together." It's ok, mother-to-be, you're eating for two as they say. It goes with the territory.

I didn't really mind because this allowed me a chance to grab a beer or two with my single buddies during football season. They always gave me the usual razzing about being a new father and being tied down but I didn't care. They were all going home to empty apartments and piles of dirty clothes along with everything else that goes with the so-called "carefree" single lifestyle.

I was going home to a well-kept house with leftovers in the refrigerator instead of TV dinners. Clean shirts and a well-made bed were also big pluses. Not to mention a pretty woman to tenderly rub my back to enhance my sleep. It didn't matter that I would be awakened later with her numerous baby questions. "That's ok, hon —stuffed pork chops for dinner sounds great," I would mutter before drifting off to dreamland once more.

Questions like, "Jim, I just know our baby will be perfect, don't you?" "Jim, if it's a boy, do you want to name him after you?" She answered this question with the statement, "I wouldn't mind, we could call him Jimmy. If it's a girl we could name her after my grandmother. She is eighty-nine, you know, and it would be her sixth great-grandchild." Funny, I hadn't even thought of that. Now I ask you—how lucky can a married man be? Questions or no questions, sleep or no sleep.

It takes nine months, or thereabouts, but the sixty-four-dollar question is finally uttered, usually in the middle of the night, "Jim, are you ready? It's time, let's go." "At last," I think to myself as I gently help her to the door. She's grimacing from pain and smiling at the same time. I'm just smiling. As I start the car I secretly hope it will be a boy because of namesake and family name. All that macho kinda stuff.

It was a girl but who cared—who really cared.

A SATURDAY WASHDAY

I was sitting at the breakfast table enjoying biscuits and white bacon gravy with Grandma and Grandpa when it started, Wump—slosh —wump—slosh. A Saturday Maytag washday at Grandma's house had begun.

I realized I would be busy today. The first day of my weekend visit. For you see, it was my job to keep the big ol' Monarch kitchen stove going to heat the wash water for the Maytag. Seems like the stove's fiery appetite was never satisfied. I swear every time I threw another piece of tamarack into its gaping mouth it seemed to roar, "Feed me, feed me!"

These thoughts made me smile as I politely stuffed another small baking powder biscuit into my mouth, smothered in white biscuit gravy, of course. My noisy stomach also seemed to growl "Feed me, feed me!"

"Hurry with your breakfast, Jimmy," Grandma said as she began to clear off the table. "You have probably guessed that today is wash day and you have work to do." "I know, Grandma," I said as I handed her my shining clean plate, wiped clean with my last biscuit. "I can hear the ol' Maytag struggling in the washroom even from here," I said with resignation in my voice.

Without hesitation I grabbed Grandpa's small hatchet from the wood box next to the stove and headed for the woodshed. No fun and games for me today till we get the wash done. Didn't really seem fair, I thought, we're not even washing my clothes.

I knew this argument wouldn't hold wash water with Grandma so I began to fill the wood box. In a way it was a pleasant chore. I always liked the smell of freshly chopped tamarack and pine, especially if it included the tart smell of pitch. This added bit of sticky goo always ended up on my hands and clothes. Just enough goo to know I had been chopping wood and packing it to the house. Another fun chore was adding bluing, a bleach and freshener product, to the water. If you weren't careful your hands would come out blue and make you grin.

Long sticky slivers of wood and bark often gathered on my arms when I carried the wood to the house. They would work their way through my sweatshirt eventually pricking my skinny nine-year-old arms. "Ouch Grandma," I said as I dumped each load into the wood box. Grandma looked down at me sternly and said, "A little hard work never hurt anyone Jimmy. Stop your bellyaching."

Then her tone changes and she added words of encouragement like, "We'll have cookies and coffee after we get donem Jimmy." "Yum," I thought. I didn't get coffee at home but Grandma felt a cup of coffee with lots of cream along with a sugar cookie or two wouldn't harm her nine-year-old grandson. To this reasoning I would smile, agree, and gently rub my waiting tummy.

The fire in the Monarch stove seemed to have a life of its own. It would get so hot with its effort to heat the wash water it seemed to breathe and pulsate.

As the washing progressed Grandma brought in a sturdy apple box from the porch and placed it next to the Maytag. Now came the fun part. I climbed up on the box and Grandma handed me the articles of wet clothing, one at a time. I then gingerly placed each one in the wringer between the turning hard rubber rollers, very carefully.

Grandma's words echoed in my ears, "Be careful, Jimmy, don't get your hands in the wringer." I can't tell you how many times she told me about the neighbor boy who got his hand caught in the wringer and it pulled his arm through the rollers, "clean up to his armpit." I knew this wasn't true because the wringer had a safety release but I always answered in my childlike voice, "I'll be careful Grandma."

It was fun to try and create different patterns of colors and shapes with the clothes as you watched them come out the dry side of the wringer. You also tried to keep them in a continuous chain. A chain that resembled my patchwork quilt Grandma had made.

After a couple of hours when the work was done we retired back to the warm kitchen and consumed our coffee and sugar cookies. She had baked the cookies the day before in anticipation of my coming visit. As I consumed my last cookie and finished my coffee with lots of cream I said, "Cookies taste better with coffee than they do with milk, don't they, Grandma?" She never failed to smile and nod her head in agreement.

The evenings on my visits to Grandmas were memorable also, when the shadows began to fall in her large living room. She would motion me to follow her as she pulled her rocking chair toward the big, black, round heating stove that sat in the center of the room. There she gathered me into her large lap and wrapped her massive grandma arms around my tiny nine-year-old torso. I can't describe the love and warmth that flowed between us but I'm sure anyone who has sat on a grandma's lap knows what I mean.

The book she would pick to read was usually the Bible, a book she knew by heart. She was a good reader and teacher even though she only had a third-grade and self-taught education, like many grandmas did in those days.

I enjoyed the stories and brightly colored pictures in the big, black book, but most of all I enjoyed her speaking about values, morals, and heaven. She always insisted we would all be together in this wonderful paradise. I never doubted her word. After all, if a grandma tells you so, it must be true.

Yes, the ol' Maytag always got the clothes squeaky clean and Grandma did her best to teach her grandson how to lead a clean life and her words, "Always be a good boy," still have a resounding effect on my life today.

Years later I inherited the ol' Maytag. It always made our washday a pleasant one, diapers and all. Thanks for the washer, Grandma, but most of all, thanks for the memories. Wump—slosh—wump—slosh—wump—slosh.

THE GLOW

"Jim, I've noticed these last few months you seem to have a warm kind of glow about you. Is something going on in your life? Did you change your diet or something?"

These questions by my work friend Larry caught me by surprise, as we enjoyed our coffee in the break room. "I was wondering if it showed," I replied in an excited voice. "I was going to keep it a secret but I guess now I will have to spill the beans." Larry leaned over the table and asked softly, "What's the secret?"

By this time I was beside myself and blurted out, "I'm going to be a father!" These words flowed from my lips with such a prideful exuberance even I was surprised. Larry almost spilled his coffee as he reached across the table and grasped my hand. It was the most heartfelt handshake I had ever experienced. His words when he spoke were so prophetic it was scary, I would realize later. "Jim, you are about to experience the consummate test of manhood and I know you are up to the challenge."

I literally glowed with pride as his words sunk in. So this is what it feels like when someone tells an expectant mother, "My dear, your pregnancy has encompassed you in its beautiful glow."

You see, all you expectant mothers out there have to understand. You don't hold a patent on "the glow." Dads can glow too.

Moms glow as they anticipate motherhood and bonding with their upcoming child. Dads glow in the knowledge that they can and will handle the added responsibility of fatherhood as expected —a task they will accomplish with tenderness, common sense, and love. Together mom and dad will make the ultimate parenthood team.

Who's kidding whom? The parenthood step in life can be scary, just like the first time your child breaks from your support and hesitantly takes his or her first unsupported step—always with childlike confidence and a smile.

Just like a child you soon learn everything in life worth obtaining is scary and risky. Your first night together, as well as marriage itself, are only starters. There's the purchase of your first home. Your first new car. Your first major calamity. Your first serious argument. Yes, I could go on and on.

You must take these steps together with loving confidence, for each of these steps will be as important as your child's first one. The step that brought a smile to that child's face and such a tender, exciting feeling to you both.

With each step your child maintains a joyful confidence and a desire for more. You also find each step into parenthood will bring you a bonding that only strengthens your love. This bonding experience will draw all of you together as a unit – it's called a family.

I can't speak for the rest of the dads in the world but I was proud of "my glow."

You see, Moms—you aren't the only ones who can glow as you await the birth of your child and motherhood. Dads can glow too.

Best of all, as the years progress and your family grows, "the glow" just keeps getting brighter and brighter and brighter.

THE BABY'S STASH

"How are we going to pay for the baby, Jim?" my wife, Lois, asked with concern in her voice. We had just received the news from the doctor about the upcoming birth of our first child. The news was met with joyful innocence—now reality was sinking in. I'm sure questions about birth expenses and how they will be paid are universal.

I had just started a new job at Sears Roebuck and had only minimal medical insurance. Lois was working only part time and had no insurance whatsoever. "Don't worry, hon," I said with confidence ringing in my voice, "I'll find a way." And indeed I did.

I paid for our first child with $2 bills. I was paid weekly. Sears paid in cash when you presented your time slip. The even dollar amount from the last $10 or close to it was always paid in $2 bills. They did this so they could determine if you were spending anything in their establishment. Even then, in the late '50s, $2 bills were scarce, with few in normal circulation. When we spent ours in the store and other places they knew we were from Sears.

We had been told the doctor bill would be $150 and the hospital bill would be $175. This figure seemed like a lot to a guy making $58.50 a week, clear. What a difference forty-five years make. The medical procedure has changed little but the monetary aspect of medical bills has become almost frightening. As the weeks progressed I would dutifully arrive home after each payday and hand Lois all my $2 bills.

She had created a secret hiding place in the cupboard where she kept our "baby stash," as she laughingly called it. I never knew where it was so I had no idea how much we were accumulating. Whenever I asked she only smiled, pointed to her now protruding stomach and said, "You will have to ask the baby." I just smiled, picked up the evening paper and said, "He doesn't feel like talking tonight." You see, I had already decided on the baby's gender. It's sort of a macho thing with males. Fortunately, wives seem to understand.

As the weeks turned into months I knew our baby stash was growing almost as fast as the baby was. The funny thing is—I never missed the money because I knew the $2 bills were not mine to keep. As in pregnancies, the delivery day finally arrived.

Awakening in the middle of the night, I reached over for Lois and she was gone, leaving a warm spot where she should have been in the bed. Then I heard her in the front room. "What's that noise?" I thought to myself, "Sounds like she is ironing." I rose up in bed and hollered to her, "What are you doing hon?" "Ironing," she said matter-of-factly. "What for?" I asked, befuddled. "It's time to go to the hospital and I want my new dress smock to look freshly pressed. Get up, grab the suitcase and go out and start the car." By the time our fourth child was born I knew this routine by heart. For you see, it never changed. The only thing that changed was the manner in which we paid for the other children. Plus our cars were newer and easier to start.

Through the years I had progressed in my career and the other children were fully covered by medical insurance. I was glad for this fact and so was Lois, but it was sad in a way. For you see, medical insurance can't cover the surprised smile on a doctor's face when you hand him a fistful of $2 bills and say, "Here's your fee, Doctor." Nor can a check from the insurance company ever take the place of Lois's baby stash and the warm feeling we both shared when I handed her my weekly $2 bills.

I had forgotten about this forty-two-year-old episode in my life until recently. I was at the supermarket when a dirty worn $2 bill was placed in my hand along with my change. A lump arose in my throat and tears came to my eyes as I gazed at its tattered corners. Our baby's stash and all it represented had arisen from my memory in a blinding flash.

Struggling with my groceries along with my memories, I walked towards my car and headed home to an empty apartment. Turning into my driveway I reflected how much fun it would be to start a baby stashs once again. Then reality set in. There isn't enough time left in my life, nor are there enough $2 bills in circulation anymore. Then I grinned as I thought – maybe, just maybe, I could start another baby stash using our new gold dollars. Dreamer.

A HOME FOR YOU AND ME AND BABIES MAKE FOUR

"Jim, it's time!" my wife exclaimed. Her normally soft voice cut the silence of the bedroom's quiet darkness like a sharp knife, bringing me to full wakefulness in seconds. After all, she was nine months and seven days pregnant with our second child. "Do you want me to call the doctor and tell him we are headed for the hospital?" I asked with both alarm and joy in my voice. "Who said anything about the hospital?" she said with a smile. "In the morning I want you to call a real estate company. It's time we buy a home."

Now all you males out there, I know, will find logic in my thought process in assuming we were on our way to the hospital. All you females out there, with a smile, will side with my wife's thoughtful logic. What better time than nine months and seven days into a pregnancy to approach a foot-dragging, house-hunting husband. One that has been in a relenting, compassionate, agreeable state for weeks, as any pregnant woman knows.

All I could think of after I sorted out her answer to my question, "Should I call the doctor?" was, "I'll call a real estate firm in the morning." With my answer locked firmly in her mind she removed her arm from my shoulder, rolled over, placing her back to me saying smugly, "I'm glad you agree it's time." At first light I was handed the phone book opened to Realtors, along with my coffee—I never had a chance.

There we were, she was nine months and eight days pregnant and I had my bankbook and briefcase in my hand as we stood nervously in front of a tall, stately, gray-haired banker. Before our interview was over I knew what it is like to totally commit to something for a long period of time. Like a thirty-year mortgage. I knew marriage would be for life but I expected a much better deal on our first house. Oh well, I thought, this will be our first and last house. You fellows know how that goes. It's like buying a boat— they just keep getting bigger and bigger as the years slip by but that's another story.

When we left the bank I knew that our loan would be approved and for how much. That was more than I knew about the sex of our soon-to-be-delivered child, or how much it would cost. The contented smile on my wife's face and the tender squeeze she bestowed upon my arm as I helped her unusually large form into the car somehow made it all worthwhile. She knew me well enough to know the hard part was over now. She had got me to the bank finally and now she could find the house, I thought, "after the baby is born."

Boy, was I wrong. At nine months and nine days she began her search. What could I do but go along? No self-respecting male would send his pregnant wife into a den of overzealous real estate salespeople alone. No disrespect intended.

I can't tell you how many places we looked at over the next few days. It was like she was on a mission and I was only the guide, a confused one at that.

All she would say as the days stretched into a week was, "I'll know our house when I see it." I had no idea what stroke of magic she would call upon to come up with such instant knowledge. It was explained to me much later quite simply, "Woman's intuition." I was told this by both my mother and mother-in-law. The only quote I could think of was the old cliché, "It's a woman's prerogative to change her mind." Neither answer brought this haggard husband any solace.

Then it happened. She started to smile as soon as I pulled up in front of a small but cozy-looking white bungalow. As she quickened her steps towards the door I heard her say to herself, "This yard will be just right for the children." Smiling, she stood impatiently in front of the door, while I fumbled for the key I had received from the real estate woman. I felt this might be the house also because I heard the saleswoman whispering something to my wife at her office. I could only hope she was lowering the price a bunch, as they had hugged each other. I asked my wife later what the saleswoman had whispered, "Believe me, intuition tells me this is the one," she replied.

My wife moved so swiftly though the sparkling, freshly painted rooms that I could hardly keep up with her. I did notice the sun shone brightly through large windows onto manicured hardwood floors. It created a feeling of warmth I hadn't experienced in the other homes we'd looked at. "Maybe there is something to this intuition business after all," I thought to myself.

We left the house about an hour later. I locked the door and we headed towards the car. As I gently helped this nine-months-and-eleven-days pregnant lady, whom I loved, into the car I asked, "Well what's the verdict?" She turned, looked at me with tears welling in her bright blue eyes and said, "This is the one." Emotionally drained myself and not trusting myself to speak, I could only nod my head in agreement.

When she awoke me that same night with a nudge and said, "Jim, it's time," I knew one thing for sure. We weren't going house hunting. It was a girl.

WHAT THE FOURTH OF JULY MEANS TO ME

The Fourth of July has meant many different things to me over the past sixty-eight years. All my perceptions were of the utmost importance at that particular moment in time.

As a child growing up the Fourth meant an all-important day off from chores, usually accompanied by a family outing, firecrackers, baked beans, bonfires and of course wieners and marshmallows on a stick.

As a draftee during a forgotten war, the Korean Conflict, the Fourth of July meant a time to serve my country. As my Dad used to say, "Your country, right or wrong, Jimmy." His logic was never questioned.

Later I would wonder why it was a forgotten war. The reasons I will never know and no one seems to care. A war was never declared nor an armistice signed. But the row upon row of white crosses bear mute testimony to its harsh reality.

Later as a father, I continued to celebrate with my family this usually warm summer holiday with the age-old traditions of my childhood. The campouts and everything that goes with these happy memorable times.

The years have progressed and the celebrations have diminished. Like in *The Winds of War* families have become more scattered due to the tugs of love and economic survival. Now with each passing year as I face my own mortality the real meaning of the Fourth of July, Independence Day, seems stronger than ever.

You have to view only the first fifteen minutes of *Saving Private Ryan* to realize the true meaning of the Fourth of July. In comparison, picture if you can Washington with his ragtag army crossing the Delaware on December 26, 1776, during a bitter cold winter that tried men's souls. Yet these two very different armies had the same ideals, love of freedom, a burning patriotic spirit, and the willingness to make unimaginable sacrifices. These same attributes symbolize all our great leaders and their armies —past and present.

These are the things I will ponder on July 4, 2000 as I unfurl my flag with pride. I will thank those who went before and those yet to come. All those who paid the price for our freedom— Happy Fourth of July.

James A. Nelson

LaVergne, TN USA
25 October 2010
202159LV00003B/163/A